LESSONS on PERFORMANCE, BUSINESS, and LIFE from a WORKING MUSICIAN

HOOKS

MATT WILSON

BROWN BOOTS PRESS

Austin, Texas

DEDICATED TO
Carter and Harry

THANK YOU

WRITING *HOOKS* HAS been one of my most challenging, rewarding, and meaningful adventures. I want to thank a handful of people who have been directly influential in bringing this book to life.

Thank you, Nicole Brogdon. *Hooks* would have been just a list of thoughts sitting in the idea bin without your encouragement and expertise.

Thank you, Tim and Angela Levy. Your knowledge, consulting, and direction made this book better. I thank you for your patience and caring for this project as if it were your very own.

Thank you to Misti Moyer for adding the final touches to the editing process. Your attention to detail, professionalism, and sincere comments were invaluable.

Thank you, Tamara Dever. TLC Book Design is the best around! Your contributions to the book, advice, and recommendations have been a Godsend!

Thank you, Mom, for answering the phone every time I needed to hear myself talk about one topic or another. Your willingness to listen and patience were immeasurable.

Thank you, Dad. The under-the-wire suggestions and proofreading were essential. I'm always grateful for your guidance and counsel.

Thank you to Lonnie, Aaron, Jim, Dan, Mark, Dave, Betsy, Ray, Kevin, and Laura. Your input was constructive and useful.

Finally, to my life-long team Mike and Laura Mordecai, Eddie and Ronda Karam, Mom and Dad, and Sarah. Thank you for the unwavering support. I am forever grateful.

CONTENTS

INTRODUCTION

DO YOU KNOW WHO I THINK I AM?

I wrote a song called "Famous" when I was a young man. The character in the song was touting his not-yet-but-certain-to-be fame that was, assuredly, right around the corner. The heading above is the first line of the song. I kind of feel that way starting this book. Do you know who I think I am?

My name is Matt Wilson. My bio says I've been a professional musician for almost thirty years now. I've played in clubs on famed streets like Bourbon in New Orleans, Sixth in Austin, and the BoardWalk at Disney World. I played the role of Piano Man in the national tour of Billy Joel and Twyla Tharp's Broadway musical *Movin' Out*. I received a resolution from the Texas State Senate for my achievements in Fine Arts. The Texas Commission on the Arts selected me for the Texas Touring Roster. I founded Matt Wilson Entertainment in 2000, offering booking, management, and performance services. From my calculation, I've made upwards of hundreds of dollars in the music business over these thirty years (wink, JK).

My greatest accomplishment is that I have been a full-time working musician since the day I graduated from college. I'm blessed and fortunate to have been able to make a living and maintain a career in music. I'm not famous like Willie Nelson. In fact, Google tells me there are other Matt Wilsons in the music business that are far more well known. Even so, I am proud of my accomplishments and aware of the effort given to achieve a life in the music business. I want to share with you what I have learned.

SOMETIMES THE ANSWER IS VERY SIMPLE

While I was standing in my kitchen one day, I noticed that a few drawers underneath the countertop were crooked. After further inspection, I realized they were actually in disrepair. Finding a little bit of time on my hands, I decided to fix this problem.

Now, lying on the floor with my tools out and my back still functioning (old man), I began to take stock of how to fix the drawers. I was familiar with the type of drawer you remove by pulling all the way out and lifting up—these were not of that sort. These drawers had a locking mechanism, extension slides, back brackets, etc. Nothing too out of the ordinary but configured in a way that I was unfamiliar. After multiple tugs and pulls, I began to unscrew. Not mentally, mind you, but literally. I started to dismantle the drawer mechanism. Only when the parts were entirely removed and separated did I see that these unfamiliar components were added for easy adjustments. I didn't need to take the drawer apart to fix it. The pieces were there to do the job for me.

That being said, with no one there to instruct me and no direction to follow, I instinctively chose to solve my drawer problem by pursuing the longest and most complicated process. All the while, the correct solution to my problem was simple and convenient.

Y'all remember in *The Karate Kid* when Mr. Miyagi had Daniel painting his fence and washing his car? Wax on, wax off! Daniel was like, "Dude! I just want to learn Karate so I can fight!"

Daniel failed to understand that the patience, focus, and fundamental movements were embedded in the mundane chores he was asked to complete. (Just like the components for my kitchen drawers were designed into the assembly for easy adjustments.)

He didn't understand, that is, until he was told. Once Mr. Miyagi revealed the secret to the instruction, Daniel discovered an efficient simplicity to learning a few Karate moves, and then he was on his way! (Rumor has it that Daniel got so good at Karate that they made a movie about him.)

Like all of us, I have repeatedly struggled with finding a lasting remedy to the same practical business concerns, onstage performance issues, discord within relationships, managing time, harnessing confidence, and silencing the doubt and fear. More times than not, my perseverance for finding relief led me to a very simple solution after years of toil and effort. A solution boiled down to its most fundamental state. A solution that could be carried out with untapped skills already in my possession.

WHAT IS A "HOOK"?

Here's a quick music lesson:

Most popular songs follow a recognizable format. Almost every tune on the radio or Spotify has a few verses, a chorus, an intro, an outro, and maybe a bridge. This traditional form of songwriting can even be found in the dustiest corners of the Library of Congress. Somewhere along the line, songwriters all agreed that this format and these elements would be universally used to create songs. The part of the song that makes it most memorable to the listener is called the hook. A hook can be played on an instrument (like the guitar intro to Guns N' Roses' "Sweet Child O' Mine") or sung (like "Sweet Caroline" by Neil Diamond). In most cases, the hook is what you remember after you listen to the song.

Many have compared life to a song. If this is true, then these ideas I share with you are the "Hooks" I've picked up along the way.

MY ONE REQUEST—CONSIDER THE NUANCE

To get the most out of this book, you must be willing to think deeper than the Hook's simplicity.

Too often, our challenges seem so difficult and complex that we assume the answers must also be.

Please take your time when reading and consider the nuance. Notice the concepts that are repetitive. These Hooks are simple. The issues they address can be quite complicated.

Now, before I cue the band, let's go back a moment.

MY STORY

My first real professional job as a musician was at Disney World. I was part of a dueling piano bar troupe at Jellyrolls on Disney's BoardWalk in Orlando, FL. I was right out of college and on top of the world. Where else could you play to a packed house every night and then walk outside to fireworks… every night?! The only problem, I was the weak link on the team when I started—by a mile!

I was always that guy in school who would wait to write the essay the night before it was due. I knew I could come up with something, and I usually did. Sure, it was B or C material, but it passed, and I paid little attention to any other detail. You could say I improvised and charmed my way through most of my life in that fashion until I jumped in at the deep end, professionally and personally.

In those days, it was standard for me to be paired onstage with a more experienced partner. Wielding little-to-no piano chops to duel, I would kill 'em with a smile. By function, the stage left piano player would control the lights with a foot switch. Early on, I recall one show where the more experienced lead stage left player ended a song by slamming his foot on the light controller and screaming, off mic in my direction, "YOU SUCK!"

HA! It's hard to charm your way out of that.

Fast forward seven years, and now I find myself onstage at the Benedum Center in Pittsburgh, PA. It never mattered how many people were in attendance to watch *Movin' Out*. I really couldn't see them in the dark, and I wasn't performing for them anyway. Of course, I wanted the paying customers to enjoy the show, but my approval needed to come from the stage managers, sound techs, dancers, and bandmates. From day one, I felt I was drowning in my desire for their approval, or lack thereof. At the end of that Pittsburgh performance, I met with the show's musical director. He wasn't too impressed. Coming from a rock 'n' roll background, I tended to be quite demonstrative when playing piano and singing. Looking back, it was probably just another way of improvising and drawing attention away from my inadequacies as a player and singer. The musical director agreed and said, "Your performance was all icing and no cake."

HA! It's hard to charm your way out of that.

By the way, my friend and stage partner who yelled, "You suck!" years ago at Disney was in attendance that night to watch my *very sweet* performance of *Movin' Out*.

Although neither recollection here serves as a watershed moment, they do reflect small snapshots that encapsulate my career. I've been fighting the "you suck" and "no substance" naysayers from the first moment I pulled down the restraint bar on this roller coaster. The one guy who has been the most persistent in championing my deficiencies lives in my head. Even after a career spanning thirty years, that dude won't let up!

The greatest lesson comes from my parents. They taught me that all things are possible and to never give up. Yes, it's cliché, but I've lived my whole life refusing to accept my limitations. The old showbiz line "Fake it till you make it" glosses over the most important lesson: you make it once you no longer need to fake it. Press on, brothers and sisters!

THE TURNING POINT

Before I could find perspective on the most defining ten years of my life, I had to lay my soul bare and come to terms with my past. I was lost and searching. Painted over so many times by persistence, ambition, and denial, an honest and fair perspective seemed improbable. Nevertheless, I had faith.

Eventually, my body and mind sensed an overwhelming need to purge this vast gamut of emotions stemming from my life's events. Physically and emotionally, I couldn't wait any longer.

Around this time is when I started my "midnight church." Unmarried, without kids, or much daytime responsibilities (I'm a musician!), I would sit down in front of my computer late at night and launch iTunes, once or twice a month, for almost three years.

Loaded with over a thousand songs and accompanied by a bottle of wine, I would call my congregation of one to order. No service was identical; however, many of the same songs and artists were called upon to work over my memories and emotions. The only light in the darkened utility room that served as my office/studio/sanctuary was the glow coming off the screen of my twenty-inch iMac.

As the wine flowed, so did the excitement. I would listen intently and study the artistic choices of famous and unheralded musicians alike. I would dance, clap, sigh, give an eye roll, yet I wouldn't sing. I was always thinking, remembering, reflecting, rejoicing, and regretting.

The music would cover a vast swath of genres and tempos, and eventually, I would always arrive in a holy place. Without fail, I would move to my favorites like Ray Charles, The Beatles, Queen, Elton, Willie, and Billy, etc.—then to the songs I sang as a young man growing up in the church.

THE MIDNIGHT PURGE

This is when the midnight purge would officially commence. The wine and song pressure washed that stoic wall shielding me from fully accepting my successes and failures until it cracked. Through that crack poured out tears that had formed years prior on Broadway stages across the country, in lonely hotel rooms in Cleveland, Tampa, Boston, LA, San Francisco, Nashville, Houston, and countless other cities. Tears set forth by the divided apartment shared with my ex-fiancé, who was on her way out. Tears brought through recognizing the seldom approval and sense of accomplishment I rarely allowed myself to feel for an unexpected, hard-won career in music, and that all-too-well-known, overwhelming fear of failure and lost opportunity. Tears recalling the joyful memories of friends and peers from my years of touring, and the constant, ever-present anxiety that served as co-pilot along the way.

Have you ever cried so much your mouth cries too? Slobber and snot. Long pauses without breath—bent over as if the Angel of Perspective was giving me the Heimlich. Oh, how I needed it!

GETTING BETTER

One night I pulled up to the computer to "have church" and realized I was empty. Perspective was finally out of my bones and on the floor. I could now begin to walk around it, pick it up. I could see these memories from different angles. I could relish the fascinating moments my life had brought me, good and bad.

This was when I started to get better. I became a better boyfriend and then, husband. I became a better singer, player, entertainer, and businessman. I eventually became a father. That perspective, those memories, the lessons that bled from my wounds gave life to a new me.

I am very blessed to have a career as a professional working musician. Considering I did not have formal training as a young man, I am proud of this accomplishment. That said, I wish I'd had formal training. The ability to rely on proper technique and education, rather than a wing and a prayer, would have served me immensely on the stages I've performed on around the world. Daily, I still see instances where a deeper knowledge of my craft would be of benefit. As a faithful man, I read:

"If an ax is dull and one doesn't sharpen it first, then one must exert more force. It's profitable to be skillful and wise." (Ecclesiastes 10:10)

CHOPPING WOOD IS EASIER WITH A SHARPENED BLADE

I've spent my entire career riding the waves of my strengths and chasing the winds of my weaknesses. Along the way, I've had to learn skills and develop tools to continue in my profession.

I can recall many instances where a thoughtful word, encouragement, or direct guidance would have helped my endeavor. My hope is that you see the practical and universal application of each of these Hooks.

Although many of these practices I share with you are my original thoughts, I have learned that I am certainly not the first to conceive these ideas. Some of what I share here, I've been told by trusted mentors and counselors. Some I have read or heard from some form of media, and I will identify those as such. In any case, I do know the majority of these thoughts and words are mine and have been crucial to my success in life and business.

Throughout, I welcome you to challenge my wisdom and to develop your own. In the end, we should strive to be content with who we are, and yet, also to have the desire and the knowledge to be better. We should long to recognize what we can offer to others and how to share. Most of all, we should aspire to live a discerning life, liberated from fear and doubt, and free to share our gifts to the world, unencumbered.

HOW TO
USE THIS BOOK

Who has time to read a book these days? I'm right there with you!

The cool thing about this book is you can read less than half of it and still find meaning. In fact, that could be your best approach. Think of *Hooks* as a reference book.

Each Hook is on a page of its own. First, I want you to read the Hook and consider how it relates to your existence before reading my "deep thoughts" on the pages that follow. Within the deep thoughts are a few sentences in bold type. The research team over here has determined that these are specific steps you can take to implement the Hook in your everyday life. As Ben Stiller says in the movie *Starsky & Hutch*, "Do it!"

Once you get a feel for how the book flows, I encourage you to write your interpretation of the Hooks using your own experiences. So, you can barely read the book at all, or you can turn it into a semi-college-class-level commitment. Your choice. Here we go!

KEY TERMINOLOGY

For those reading who are not in the music business, below is a not-so-thorough key to help the conversation relate to your adventures and endeavors. My stage time is similar to your meeting presentation, and so on.

Performance = presentation, talk, show, act, speech, crucial conversations, meaningful conversations, arguments, sales pitch

Musician/Artist = speaker, presenter, actor, dancer, counselor, any craft that involves performing or presenting something to an audience or group

Stage = dais, podium, office, meeting room

Song = idea, book, thesis, presentation, message

PERFORMANCE

*How to prepare and perform your best
when it matters most*

HOOK #1

The audience rarely notices the flaw that consumes the artist.

I MET MY wife while on tour with *Movin' Out*. She was a dancer in the show. Now she is climbing the corporate ladder in the hotel business.

That said, she still keeps an eye on the dance world and hasn't forgotten all of the technique she learned for so many years as a professional dancer. Every now and then, we will sit together and watch a ballet or some sort of dance performance on TV. (I'm a fantastic husband!) Occasionally, she will say "Oh" or "Oops" or something along those lines. This is the most fascinating part of our time together in these moments. She is watching the performance with a trained eye. She can see the flaws and the perfection. She is moved by the delivery and the mistakes. I am not a trained dancer. (Even though many at Robert T. Hill Middle School were mesmerized by my Roger Rabbit!) I do not see the intricacies of the performance and technique.

Truth be told, no one else does either (relatively speaking). Sure, it's essential as an artist to hit your mark consistently. However, spectators don't want a stressed-out ballerina fretting over the awkward arabesque. They want a happy, engaged, competent, and confident performer. They want an experience! For all they know, an arabesque is a bird or something.

A few years ago, I was asked to perform a show with a large gathering of local musicians. I really wanted to contribute and establish my worth as an artist in the community. I placed so much meaning on the show and its outcome that I set myself up for a struggle. When it was my solo, I briefly let my anxiety get the better of me. I called on my years of stage experience to cover my fear and flaws; however, I was freaking out! After the show, I was embarrassed and ashamed. I hated that I allowed my anxiety to rob me of my ability to thrive in such an exciting moment. For days, I allowed myself to wallow in disappointment and failure.

I decided to reach out to a close friend of mine who was in the audience. I was very open with her about my fear and asked her, "How bad did it show?" (I was certain it showed!) She told me she didn't notice anything at all, and in her opinion, my songs were the highlight of the night! She happened to record some video of my performance and sent it to me. It wasn't bad. In fact,

I chose to share it via social media. (This is our new standard folks!) Relieved, I was sort of proud of it.

Don't get me wrong, I would take a *do-over* if given a chance. I'm sure I missed an opportunity to make a better impression on some of my peers. However, the audience experienced the overall performance. They were not listening for my errors. They wanted me to succeed, and from their point of view, I did. I would have had a little less anxiety in the show if I had welcomed their acceptance from the beginning.

Sure, we can aim for perfection. Yet, we all need to learn when to be ok with what we perceive to be "less than." It's counterproductive to waste time and energy brooding over a small, minor detail that no one noticed or will notice.

I lost a few days of joy and happiness ruminating over that "bad" performance. I was sure everyone could hear my flat notes and sense my inner turmoil. They couldn't and they didn't.

HOOK #2

Mental preparation for high-pressure performances should begin early.
Learn how to prepare mentally.

ANY ENDEAVOR THAT calls for precise performance requires preparation and practice.

Most likely, the associate who is giving a presentation to the board practices her speech in some form. A band calls a few rehearsals before the big show. A sports team holds practices and meetings to prepare for the big game. Groundbreaking insight here, I know!

However, the preparation for the speech should not just be in reciting the words on the page. The ramp-up to the big show should not only be the execution of the notes on the staff. The game is not just about physically delivering the ball.

Jimmy Johnson is one of the most successful football coaches in the history of the game. Often, he would say to his players, "Let the mind control the body, not the body control the mind."

One's ability to have a clear and free mind is the first step to a successful performance.

Focus is a skill strengthened by practicing techniques such as meditation, positive thinking, visualization, and coaching. Training your mind on what to focus on (and when) can be the very thing needed for optimal performance.

Always prepare physically and mentally!

HOOK #3

Pay attention to how you react when presented with an opportunity. Initial, unmanaged reactions could eventually lead to disappointment.

MANY ARE FAMILIAR with the quote, "Luck is when preparation meets opportunity."

Often, we aim our preparation toward an unseen, nonspecific moment. We carry on, maintaining our daily lives, while we wait for elevating opportunities, personally and professionally. How we initially react when that elevating opportunity finally comes along will contribute to determining the outcome.

Many years after leaving *Movin' Out*, I was invited to audition for another touring Broadway show. I was still struggling a bit from focusing too much on my past Broadway disappointments rather than the successes (more on that later in Hook #20), so I was excited but apprehensive. I dreaded feeling the sting of performance anxiety in a pressure situation again. I was concerned the "Broadway thing" would trigger an uncontrolled performance. However, I was prepared. I understood my body and my mind way better than years before. I circled my team and talked it out. I prepared mentally and physically for the audition. I didn't get the part. (No big deal. I think I was too old.) I did make a great impression, however. My manager told me I was one of two in the citywide audition that stood out. More importantly, I wasn't in turmoil. I was in control. I'm not sure that would have been the case if I were not in tune with my emotions and reactions beforehand.

Pay attention to your reactions to a new endeavor, especially if anxiety and uncertainty accompany the excitement. **You will need to examine your reactions, understand them, and prepare to manage them before taking on your task.**

These thoughts and feelings won't go away unattended. In fact, they will emerge at the most inopportune moments.

Take comfort in knowing that simply being aware of your mental state is a giant step in managing whatever reactions arise. It's easier to regulate an emotion when it's identified.

For example, if a new opportunity brings apprehension and some fear, accept it and admit it. Then ask why. Try to understand the source of the fear or discomfort. Now you have time to work on alleviating the specific parts of your endeavor causing the uncertainty.

See, this is crucial because now you can prepare for a burden that, undoubtedly, you must shoulder. **When we are caught unaware by our emotions, we are then tasked to cope with two separate reactions:** "I'm anxious right now! Why am I anxious? The fact that I'm anxious is making me anxious!"

My anxiety was high during my time in *Movin' Out* (Hook #53). Eventually, rather than fighting it, I just accepted it. I knew the uncomfortable feelings would find their way into my performance. Rather than hoping that "this time I won't be anxious performing that one song," I just accepted that my body was *gonna do what it was gonna do* (anxiety is not rational, and most times, you can't just "think it away"). **Removing the shock and identifying the emotion made a world of difference.**

There's a saying in sports, "You can't play injured, but you can play hurt." I viewed my anxiety as playing "hurt." I was able to manage the pain because I admitted it was there. This is a lesson that has served me well.

OPPORTUNITY REACTION MANAGEMENT SYSTEM

Next time you are worried about a new opportunity, try out this super scientific-sounding process:

1. **Identify the uncertainty.** Be very specific!

2. **Ask, "What if?"** Go wild here. Allow yourself a moment to explore whatever it is you think could go wrong. Visualize the enemy!

3. **Make a plan.** Now that you know what you are concerned about and how it may unfold, formulate a counterstrategy. This will include practicing, reviewing skill techniques, strengthening your focusing processes, and setting/following a routine.

4. **Move into a position of control.** You have a say in what happens. Gain confidence from executing your plan. Your preparation will not be in vain.

5. **Go.** It's time. It's your turn. Do the thing. Apply the WASH technique (Hook #18).

6. **Accept the outcome.** Acknowledge that, if you followed the first five steps earnestly, then you gave it your best. If not good enough, then you need to get better. Disappointing, sure, but no shame in realizing you need more work. Getting better is always attainable. On the flip side, if you are satisfied with the result, then congratulations! It worked!

HOOK #4

In pressure performance, your "Base Level" ability will manifest.

FIRST OFF, "BASE level" is a geological term defined as "the lowest level to which running water can flow and erode." We will come back to that.

There is a saying: "Don't practice until you do it right. Practice until you can't do it wrong."

For many, showcasing a skill, like playing an instrument or giving a public presentation, can be a daunting task. Along with the fundamental charge to execute, there is often a perceived pressure that accompanies the effort. When the room is full, the decision-makers are watching, and the lights are bright, most will need to ward off distraction (positive and negative). You can only rely on how you have trained your mind and body to react. How will you deliver through the potentially sweaty palms, shortness of breath, tight muscles, and incessant inner speech? These things don't have to derail you!

Let's think of these distractions as water and your ability to perform as the ground. The "water" (distractions) will wear down the "ground" (your ability to perform) until it reaches the base level. The "ground" that remains is your Base Level.

"Reinforce your Base Level through practice and preparation. You will showcase that level more than you realize."

Your Base Level is essentially the lowest level of your performance ability (not including being hindered by a substance or limited by injury, etc.). Bluntly stated, when really trying, your Base Level is as bad as it will get in any normal circumstance! Your ground (ability) will hold no matter the flood (distractions).

Reinforce your Base Level through practice and preparation. You will showcase that level more than you realize.

Yes, we always aim to perform at an optimal and inspired level. However, often we are only able to perform at our Base Level. When we hear of performers or athletes performing "in the zone," it is usually referring to a level above their norm. Michael Jordan scored sixty-three points in a playoff game in 1986. He was "in the zone." Of course, he didn't do that every game. Most certainly, there are myriad of distractions in a basketball season. However, his Base Level was consistently better than everyone else's. That is why he is considered the greatest basketball player of all time. (LeBron is great, but I'm in the Jordan camp!)

If you practice to raise your Base Level and find progress, you are getting better. No matter what state you are in emotionally, or what circumstances surround the performance, a strong Base Level will increase your ability for consistent success.

There will be a flood. Shore your ground!

HOOK #5

*In pressure performance,
your body will respond
like a machine.
Learn its buttons and levers.*

THIS HOOK RELATES to the Base Level Theory introduced a few pages back.

I used to struggle with singing flat. I worked hard at correcting this issue and, thus, raised my Base Level for singing. Along the way, I realized that physically I had developed counterproductive habits. By learning where to draw support and where to release tension, I improved the quality of my singing.

Train your body how you want it to react and it will. Consider that you can find countless articles, books, podcasts, and websites dedicated to understanding and improving a variety of abilities:

- Public Speaking
- Singing
- Playing an Instrument
- Athletic Performance
- Controlling Focus
- Maintaining Composure
- Proper Posture
- Better Sleep
- Breathing (most important)

The list rolls on. As the good book says, "Seek, and you shall find."

Your muscles seem to have a "mind of their own"—you know, muscle memory. Teach your muscles how to function as if they were a separate entity capable of receiving instruction. You can do this by practicing a specific movement or action. (Truthfully, your muscles do not have "minds of their own." Octopuses have brains in their arms; we don't. Your muscle memory is stored mainly in the brain in your head. However, for our purposes in *Hooks*, we will rely on the imagery of building muscle memory through practice, repetition, and programming. Onward!)

When learning a new song, sometimes I will practice the more difficult piano passages while watching TV or listening to the radio. True, this is not the most focused and ideal form of practice. However, I envision teaching my fingers the repetitive motion and order of the passages. It works for me!

You can also learn from watching others. There are tricks to fortifying muscle memory long term. Just as one learns how to play the guitar or operate a machine, your body is an instrument and can be given the same attention and approach.

Sometimes when I'm performing, I sense I'm losing control of my ability to focus. These distracting thoughts often begin to affect my performance. So, I'll divert my thoughts simply to get out of my own way (Hook# 52). I'll force myself to think of something completely unrelated to the task at hand just so my body can do what I trained it to do. In these moments, the only thing affecting my ability to perform freely is my mind.

I'm drawn to the simple task of tying a shoe. I would assume that many of us can tie a shoe even under the most stressful and dire of situations. We maintain the ability to "tie the shoe" because it's been ingrained in our fingers, hands, arms, and brain. We've repeated our technique of tying a shoe a million times. (Btw, have you ever seen someone tie their shoe differently than you? Weird!) It's hard to mess up tying a shoe!

I can hear Rip Torn's character in the movie *Dodgeball*: "If you can dodge a wrench, you can dodge a ball!"

So, if you can tie your shoe, you can play piano. Or sing in tune. Or give a speech. Or...

HOOK #6

Practice to raise your Base Level.

AGAIN, BASE LEVEL is the level in which one performs under duress or distraction.

Not too long ago, I encountered something unfamiliar in my career: being the "new kid in town." My wife was offered a promotion that required a transfer. I began building my career in Austin during college, so I was initially apprehensive about starting anew in New Orleans. Knowing I'd be close to Texas and could easily shuttle back-n-forth greased my wheels. (Of course, the word PROMOTION carried a little bit of weight also.)

The only times in my life I moved to a new city were right out of high school and then college. The move from high school to college doesn't really count ('cause, whatever), and the move from The University of Texas to Orlando sort of counts. I figure it to be a rite of passage to move somewhere new when you are young.

I also moved, briefly, to New York and South Carolina for work. But I wasn't *new* because they asked me to be there. So, there I was, in this not-so-common position of being a new guy in a new town as a middle-aged man. I found it to be liberating, refreshing, and challenging.

The challenge was that each opportunity carried somewhat significant weight. Every performance offered a chance to establish a new reputation, good or bad.

I welcomed this challenge. However, I noticed it brought a new set of distractions and concerns. Each venue and scene had its own expectations and procedures. You want to impress but also fit in.

The fact that I'd honed my performance technique and prepared for a variety of venues served me quite well in this instance. While listening to my internal monologue ponder such things as "Does this sound good?", "Is this what they normally do?", "Why is that guy looking at me weird?" (by the way, I do this because I'm human), my Base Level of performance chugged along at a professional standard.

I wasn't perfect by any means, yet I noticed I was not making the same errors I was prone to make in similar past situations. Through patience, persistence, and practice, I'd been rewarded with a higher Base Level of performance ability.

Back in Texas, I can recall starting a show and immediately noticing the sound system malfunctioning. (To the point where I had to explain the issue to the crowd.) After that issue was resolved, I noticed some of my equipment onstage wasn't working properly either. I fixed that. Yet, these distractions affected the natural flow of the show. So, I was doing my best to make a good first impression on the audience, despite the troubles, and guide the show in a controlled direction.

"...but having developed a strong Base Level, mentally and physically, I was able to deliver."

One distraction followed another. All the while, I could feel my mind and body wanting to react negatively. Because of my training, I was able to identify what was needed to calm my body (my instrument) so I could play and sing at a professional level. The distractions made this difficult, but having developed a strong Base Level, mentally and physically, I was able to deliver.

Don't get caught off guard not knowing how you respond under pressure. Know your Base Level and work to make it better.

HOOK #7

Don't show them what you can't do.

EVERY *MOVIN' OUT* performance closed with the song "New York State of Mind." At the very end of the tune, the part called for me to improvise vocally and on the piano. The desired effect was an off-the-cuff, dramatic conclusion to the song and the show. I had the piano chops to show off a little bit, but vocally, I had to limit my exposure. One night, my excitement led me to a vocal riff I had no business attempting. Our musical director pulled me aside after the show and said, "You were doing great until you blew it with that vocal improv."

I had to agree. I showed them what I couldn't do!

"Showcase your strengths onstage."

My dear friend and first true musical mentor, Ray McGee, reminded me of this Hook many times. **Limit your weaknesses to the rehearsal room. Showcase your strengths onstage.** Most times, your audience will not know what you believe they are missing.

HOOK #8

Warm up.
Cool down.

EARLY ON IN my career, one of my managers said I should "cool down" vocally after my shows and rehearsals. I was aware of the warm-up process because it was physically obvious and made sense. At the time, I brushed off the cool-down advice as pointless.

Fast forward many years. I developed a small nodule on my vocal cord. My treatment was speech therapy. Of course, my therapist confirmed my belief in the warm-up process. Then she said, "No matter what you do to your voice during a performance, don't leave it there. Use cool-down exercises to put the voice back in its natural, unstressed place. This will help prevent long-term damage."

I often hear public speakers, salespeople, teachers, counselors, or anyone required to use their voice a lot, struggle with a tired voice. (Singers are not the only ones who could use a warm-up and cool-down.)

In the moments following a strenuous performance, allow time to settle your voice, mind, and body back into a place of rest.

Try the following exercise to reset your voice after an arduous speech or performance, a long day on the phone and in meetings, a full day of teaching, or a rough Sunday afternoon watching your favorite football team:

1. Find a drinking straw and cut it in half.

2. Gently blow into the straw five times.

3. Set the straw down. Place your hands on your cheeks. Gently massage and say "ha ha ha" three times. Place the "ha's" in your normal speaking range and at average speaking volume.

4. Remove your hands from your cheeks, and then, in normal range and volume, say "FWAY" three times.

Repeat this process until you have reset your voice and calmed your mind.

While we are on topic, I would also like to offer a few thoughts on warming up. **Whereas the cool-down is easy to neglect because no one**

really considers the benefit, the warm-up is often neglected simply because we are lazy. Most of us who dismiss the warm-up, in whatever profession, are the ones who've been around a while and carry the attitude of "I got this!"

"A more subtle reason to warm up is to protect the performer's fickle state of confidence."

Obviously, an athlete warms up to prevent injury. And a singer or speaker facing a loud and aggressive performance or speech should ease their way in to avoid damage to the voice. However, a more subtle reason to warm up is to protect the performer's fickle state of confidence.

As I reference in Hook #19, confidence comes from demonstrated ability. The opposite can also be true. Confidence can be lost from poorly demonstrated ability.

Think of any situation (a game, a discussion, singing a song, giving a speech) where you said or thought, "Do it again; I wasn't ready." The implication here is that if you were ready, you would do it better. In essence, you are saying, "Don't judge me on that effort. I'm better than that when I'm ready to go!"

Ok, so we spend our lives perfecting our craft through practice and training. This training leads us to opportunities for presentation to the public, and we meet our expectations. We then gain confidence that we can do this thing and do it well. We get so good at it that we forgo the preparation once needed to deliver.

That's when the foundation cracks ever so slightly. Without some pre-show vocal exercises, the singer's voice feels rigid and awkward, and the audience can tell. The speaker's mind and mouth aren't in sync because no moment was taken before the speech to review the notes or rev up the "speaker" voice. And the audience can tell. The obvious one, the bullpen pitcher serves up a meatball because he didn't adequately follow his warm-up routine before entering the game. And the opposing batter can tell. HOMERUN!

Now the performer, speaker, or pitcher is left with the lingering cloud of failure and disappointment. Sure, the thoughts can be dismissed with the ol' "I wasn't ready." Yet, in truth, a little doubt will creep in, even if only for a brief moment. **Again, confidence can be lost from poorly demonstrated ability.**

Doubt and lack of confidence can be devastating at times. Why even play around with it? Warm up! Give yourself the best chance to succeed. Protect your mind and your body.

HOOK #9

*Perform the show
you were hired to perform.
If you don't agree
with the direction,
don't take the gig.*

IN 2010, I expanded my entertainment services to include booking and show management. Clients come and go; however, at any given time, I am now responsible for booking a handful of regional clubs and private events.

One matter I frequently encounter with musicians, venue owners, and clients centers around show direction. Often, the musician's idea of how a show should be performed does not match what the purchaser wants. Sometimes I agree that the purchaser's, owner's, or manager's vision is misguided. I also trust most of my musicians on what is appropriate for each situation.

However, I always remind my players that we are hired to play the show requested. If they strongly disagree, then they shouldn't take the gig. It's that simple. Of course, things might change if there is an opportunity for discussion. **Otherwise, the rule is, "Play the show they paid you to play."**

"In all types of industry, professionals are asked to target their services to meet the specific needs of their clients."

This idea permeates throughout the business world. In all types of industry, professionals are asked to target their services to meet the specific needs of their clients. The book you are reading now is a perfect example.

The team I hired to consult on the manuscript, design, and publishing of *Hooks* created a blueprint for "how to write a book." In fact, the owner of the company actually wrote a book on how to write a book (*The Fast Book Handbook* by Tim Levy). To meet my specific vision for *Hooks*, I asked to make some changes to the standard blueprint. After some consideration, the team cheerfully obliged, and we were on our way. They could have easily said, "No, this is not how we do things," or been difficult along the way. That didn't happen. They evaluated my requests, determined they could oblige, and got to work. (So, if you have problems here, blame me! HA!)

I recall talking to a fellow band leader about playing original music on cover band, private party performances. My stance at the time was, "I'm an artist, and I'm gonna get my music out whenever I can." Not a bad way to approach things. However, my friend said, "I let go of that years ago. They are hiring us to play songs everyone knows, and they want to dance. Unless everyone knows your tunes, then it's probably not the right time or setting to showcase your original material."

This hit home. If I really want to play my original tunes, I should find venues that welcome that direction. Otherwise, I should play "Don't Stop Believin'" with the enthusiasm of a weekend karaoke singer.

If you are hired to perform a service or task, do what you were hired to do. If you disagree with the direction or cannot accommodate, decline. (More on this in Hook #10.)

HOOK #10

It's their party, not your concert.

IT'S BENEFICIAL TO understand and accept the purpose of each performance, project, or job.

Most musicians would prefer to play for an attentive and appreciative audience. However, many times, that is not the purpose of the entertainment. Sometimes the purpose is simply background music for a cocktail party or high energy dance music for a wedding.

Insisting on forcing your artistry or agenda on someone who hires you for a different purpose is unprofessional and selfish. If the client wants the music softer, then turn it down. If the client wants the company's CEO to sing "Livin' On A Prayer" with the band and the head of marketing to play percussion, let them do it! **Clients will always remember a cooperative and agreeable band before they remember a brilliant musician.**

One of my artists was hired to perform at a corporate function. The client was quite particular about the setup and staging area. (So extreme that they prevented him from having water onstage during his performance. Hardcore!) As the demands continued to roll in, I counseled my artist just to say yes. Unfortunately, a situation arose that altered the entire event, and my artist didn't perform. However, he was so agreeable and flexible to their needs and wishes, they praised his willingness to accommodate and placed him on their preferred vendor list—without him singing or playing a single note!

A venue manager once asked me to "turn down" a closed baby grand piano (with no amplification) during a performance. Truthfully, there was not much I could do to make this acoustic instrument any quieter, other than barely press the piano keys. So, I smiled and agreed to "turn it down." They preferred to have music that no one could hear. I gladly obliged!

When you can be versatile with your product without sacrificing quality, you open yourself to *more* opportunities. Also, when you can home in on the service requested, and then stay within those boundaries, you open yourself to *repeat* opportunities.

When contracted for a specific purpose, aim to be versatile and accommodating.

HOOK #11

*Stage banter–
it really doesn't matter
what you say, as long as
it's said clearly, with conviction,
and confidence.*

I AM OFTEN in a position to offer guidance to new performers and speakers who want direction with improvised stage banter. I define stage banter as the passing thoughts in between the intended message of the presentation or performance. Having the ability to talk onstage in an easygoing and comfortable manner is of tremendous benefit to a show or presentation. (For this point, I am not referring to scripted shows.)

I don't perceive talking to an audience to be any different than speaking to someone directly.

- I want to be informative (what song am I singing, or what's the point of the show, etc.).
- I want to be enthusiastic and positive.
- I want to be receptive, and
- I want to be charming or humorous when appropriate.

I believe what you say is less important than the confidence with which you say it. Not everything you say has to be funny or entertaining. Conversations are made up of points and passing thoughts. The same is true of stage banter. Sometimes the inspiration is there for wit and emotion. Sometimes you are just buying time until the dessert arrives, if you will.

Say something. Say it clearly so we can understand you. Say it loud enough so we can hear you. Say it with confidence.

At that point, it won't really matter that you just told us about getting a haircut as you segue into the next song, slide, or topic.

HOOK #12

Edgy performance banter
that entertains ten
and offends one
is probably not worth it.
There's always a better way.

I KNOW PLENTY of performers who disagree with me on this point of view.

Even so, I believe the fleeting gain you will receive from being offensive in the name of humor is far outweighed by the potential loss of a customer, follower, or listener.

Someone will quickly forget your crude joke if they find it funny. However, they will remember it forever if it _justifiably_ offends them.

(Excuse me. Please make room for my soapbox.)

I also believe vulgar humor is base and low hanging fruit. Although sometimes funny or well placed, "blue" banter typically requires the least amount of creativity and is the most used tool of the inexperienced performer.

Offensive, mind you, doesn't have to mean just crude or vulgar. Being overly aggressive or demeaning to your audience can also be offensive.

Once, I encountered a challenging group at one of my all-request piano shows. While sitting directly in front of the stage, they insisted on talking loudly and refused to respond to my entertainment in an acceptable manner. How dare they!

"Yes, I believe there is a way to be entertaining without being offensive."

Sidenote, one large section of unruly guests will sour any performance in a showroom, theater, or hall. The old showbiz adage is, "Before you can pull the rug out from underneath an audience, you must first get them to stand on the rug." Unruly folks don't stand on no rugs!

Anyway, after a few subtle attempts to get them in line, I decided to go after them aggressively. Trying to maintain a humorous tone, I repeatedly called them out and insisted they change their rebellious ways. Once I sensed I crossed the line, I backed down and tried to play nice. Not until after the show did I realize my overly aggressive approach resulted in a slew of unflattering reviews online. The reviews were harsh, personal, and consequently, reflected poorly on the venue. The next few days consisted of phone calls and emails cleaning up the mess I'd made.

When it was all said and done, I reminded myself that there was a better way! I could have gone about things in an entertaining and engaging manner while also maintaining integrity.

Yes, I believe there is a way to be entertaining without being offensive.

HOOK #13

Don't blame the audience when they don't know what you want them to do.

ONE OF THE entertainers I studied under had a great line. On nights where eliciting a response from the crowd was difficult, he would say, "I'm sure you are all wonderful people individually. However, all together, you make a terrible audience!" HA!

It's a common occurrence; sometimes, the "tried and true" just doesn't work. Your jokes fall flat, or the best songs don't *get 'em going* like the night before. Some audiences are not prepared or in the mood to be entertained.

That said, I have come to accept that it's my job to put the audience in the right frame of mind. Too often, I hear performers say, "I tried all my regular bits and nothing worked. That crowd was lame! Nothing we could do!"

Maybe so, but if as a performer, you have already determined that you are going to execute a particular show no matter what, then you might be in for disappointment and failure.

A seasoned performer will "read the room." They'll know when to leave out a joke or add more. Know when to get to the point quickly or delay the message a bit. Know when to play the hits.

I try to emphasize that a good part of my value as an entertainer is my ability to read a room. I know it's one of my strengths. Not being able to *feel the room* or connect with the audience is like driving blind.

Also, accepting that each audience can be entertained puts you in a place of meeting the challenge. Rather than, "I gave 'em my stuff, and they didn't respond," one should consider, "What can I do differently to encourage these folks to enjoy this moment?"

The same can be true for product. I released a record in 2005 called *Revolving Doors*. The name referred to my living situation while touring: on the road and living in hotels (some of which had revolving doors). The purpose of the CD cover was to introduce new listeners to Matt Wilson and attract their attention to the point of buying a disc. My idea for the cover was to use a photo of me walking through a revolving door. The image we chose showed just that, from the waist down. So, I released a record with my butt on the cover (and not my face) to a public who wouldn't recognize me even if they were sharing the said revolving door. No wonder I'm not hounded for autographs!

Whether it's your product or your presentation, accept the idea that your audience wants to be satisfied and informed. It's your responsibility alone to give them a clear and resonant experience. While I was writing *Hooks*, one of my mentors would reiterate, "Do the work for the reader, *join the dots*."

When starting a new project or addressing an audience, a review of the following should set you in the right direction:

1. **Identify the purpose of your presentation or product.** Who is your audience? Do you want them to learn, laugh, cry, sit still and listen, buy something, participate? (If you are a musician, do you want someone to recognize you after they buy your CD?)

2. **Choose a delivery strategy.** Are you going to attempt humor, tell stories, sing songs, or get right to business? What's the best way to package and sell your product? (If you are a musician making a CD, are you going to use an image on the cover?)

3. **Be prepared to pivot.** Your goals should be defined and pursued in earnest. However, a good product or presentation can be hindered by a misguided strategy. Successfully changing course is the mark of a professional. (For example, if you are a musician making a CD with an image on the front cover, and you showed a picture of your butt walking through a door, do something else next time.)

Accept responsibility for your successes and failures. Show 'em your good side, not your backside!

HOOK #14

Separate the importance of the performance from the skill required to deliver the performance.

HERE'S A COMMON scenario: It's a cold Tuesday night in January and Freddie "Piano Man" O'tan has a gig at the local steakhouse. He's played this venue a hundred times or more. He knows the staff and knows the clientele. They like him, and he likes them. He knows the equipment and the perfect mix for the room. He knows when to order his complimentary meal that fits perfectly within the allotted budget for musicians. At the end of the night, he knows who to ask for payment and in what form it will come. This is a low-pressure situation for Freddie, and he knows it.

Here's another common scenario: It's a Saturday night in October. Freddie and his band have been asked to play the largest and most popular event in the city. It's a fundraiser with local and national bigwigs (some famous musicians) scheduled to attend. The band has never played the venue before, so they will need to navigate the venue's load in and soundcheck for the first time. Freddie's production team is one of the best. Still, they will need to mix an unfamiliar room. Since it's Freddie's band, he is in charge. He must make sure everyone is on time and knows where to load in and then park. He must make sure that the band is aware of the timeline and remind them to stay close in case things change. (The timeline always changes!) Where is the green room!? Freddie absolutely must have the band's dinner accommodations organized. A hungry band is a mad and bad band. Freddie must also have the song list in mind. What are they going to play and when? The group that hired Freddie's band heard great things and has high expectations. This is a high-pressure performance. A good show might mean future opportunities with the client and some attention from influential people in attendance.

> ### "The only thing standing in the way of Freddie performing to his best level is what he allows to be distracting."

Both scenarios here share one thing in common, and it's this most important thing: At some point after all the gear has been set up and the cars parked (or not). After the band has arrived, stomachs full, and are in good spirits (or not). After the production team has mixed the room, just so, and the sound is on point (or not). Then the moment will finally arrive for Freddie to approach his instrument and play.

What is ultimately required at that moment is the same whether Freddie is at the steakhouse or the convention center. Professional musician Freddie must play his instrument professionally. For the focus here, the only thing standing in the way of Freddie performing to his best level is what he allows to be distracting.

Will Freddie play a little sloppy and loose at the steakhouse? No big deal, right? Will Freddie tense up and let his nerves get the best of him at the fundraiser? It's such a BIG DEAL, right? **Not if he approaches both performances equally.**

It's a matter of perspective. Let's move to the next Hook.

HOOK #15

Perspective is a powerful tool. Deliberately focus your lens.

PERSPECTIVE IS DEFINED as "a particular attitude toward or way of regarding something; a point of view."

Continuing with the scenarios laid out in Hook #14, if Freddie can control his perspective, he will perform each gig the same.

Sure, the steakhouse gig has few ramifications and requires almost no effort compared to the fundraiser. However, if Freddie is too unfocused, plays poorly, takes long breaks, maybe is a little late here and there, then Freddie won't have that gig anymore.

Ok, fine! The fundraiser has a ton of ramifications and requires a lot of effort compared to the steakhouse gig. Yet, if Freddie is too burdened with the mental weight of the opportunity and the effort required to play freely, then he may not get that gig anymore.

The solution here is for Freddie to control his perspective and approach both performances the same way. The G chord he will play at the steakhouse will require the same fingering, timing, and velocity as it will at the fundraiser. (Ok, maybe a bit quieter at the steakhouse. People are trying to have dinner!) The piano doesn't "know" the difference.

Freddie will most likely remember how, when, and where to place his feet on the pedals to drive his car to the gigs and do this consistently. He will most likely remember how to navigate the stairs to get onstage. The percentages are high that Freddie will remember how to take in enough breath, manipulate his mouth, remember the words to greet his bandmates, and have pre-show conversations at an appropriate volume. All of these tasks are routine yet are still required to execute the show. If Freddie forgets how to talk, or forgets how to drive and crashes, or can't get onstage, then there's a problem.

The point is, the components of a skill learned to the level of professional quality are both mental and physical. Our perspective (mental approach) will often interfere and impede our ability to perform at our best. Freddie's ability to talk before the show is free and on point. His execution is flawless. He's "killing it" talking to his band! Why? Because he's not thinking about it.

There's no consideration to assign value to this function, good or bad. He's taught his body how to do something, and he's letting it happen.

Freddie's focus (perspective) on each gig should be on the instrument, music, and his performance. When his perspective is controlled and focused inward, he will play to his optimal level and be consistent. When his focus is outward (the distractions), his ability to perform will be hindered and inconsistent.

> *"Your body is your instrument.*
> *Focus inward on playing your instrument*
> *to the best of your ability,*
> *no matter the setting."*

This idea on performance perspective can be applied to boardrooms, sales meetings, presentation theaters, and dinner tables alike. No matter how much or how little is on the line, the specific physical requirements to deliver your presentation remain the same. Your body is your instrument. Train, practice, and learn how to use your instrument. Raise your Base Level (Hook #6). Focus inward on playing your instrument to the best of your ability, no matter the setting. Then, go do your thing!

Let's add to this in the next Hook.

HOOK #16

Reserve assigning value to any significant situation. Good is not always good, and bad is not always bad.

I REMEMBER HAVING a conversation with my dad a few days after I landed the role in *Movin' Out*. Within all the excitement, he said, "You may never have to worry about finding work again." Caught up in the moment, I agreed! I also believed the accomplishment would alleviate many of the doubts and insecurities I carried up to that point. Getting the part was good and was going to continue to be good. Good all around for everyone! I was wrong.

Don't misunderstand; my time as the Piano Man was life changing. It has been a calling card professionally for years, and rightly so. When I allow myself to feel rewarded for my accomplishments, I might even gain a little confidence here and there from my time on Broadway. (I am my worst critic, so it's difficult for me to reward myself. Who here is with me? 'Sup fam!)

Truthfully, life in the show wasn't all good. It was tough at times. There were moments I struggled personally and professionally. I still carry fragments of that turmoil to this day. I've been blessed to work consistently since I left the tour. However, *Movin' Out* wasn't my life-long lottery ticket. In retrospect, my professional insecurities were intensified. They certainly didn't go away as I envisioned.

Many years after the tour, bluntly stated, I was fired from a local gig. At the time, it was difficult for me to understand, and I viewed the matter as negative. My perspective now allows me to see that it was quite positive and one of the most important happenings in my career. I needed a change at the time. I needed a fresh start. I needed some time to evaluate my performances and ability. All of these good things wouldn't have happened without the bad thing happening first.

"When we weigh something as good or bad, we can simply be wrong."

When we weigh something as good or bad, we can simply be wrong. When we put that weight (the sandbag of good or bad) on something (performance, relationship, interaction, opportunity) before the fact,

we are then possibly giving that something too much importance and meaning. And thus, we are preventing that moment or event to unfold freely.

Back to Freddie "Piano Man" O'tan. If Freddie just plays his shows like he is trained and allows the results to fall as they may, he will more than likely have sustained success. The success will come from his patience and persistence, his practice, and willingness to give what is needed to be a professional. Of course, he must be good enough and capitalize on his opportunities. Yet, no matter the outcome, at least he will not get in his own way by attributing burdensome value to his situation.

I read a book on mindfulness. The one thing I remember most was this, "Life is cooking dinner, eating the meal, and then cleaning your bowl."

Keep things simple, follow your routine, hone your skills, and just play your instrument.

Let life unfold along the way.

HOOK #17

Positive and negative emotion can adversely affect performance.

WE CAN ALL relate to a situation where we find ourselves performing a task under the watchful gaze of an audience (giving a speech, swinging a golf club, performing a show), and thoughts of doubt and failure creep in. Often, these thoughts and emotions can completely derail our efforts, or at the very least, slightly cause a hiccup and interrupt our flow. What many don't realize is that positive emotions can do the same.

We are at our best when we are not evaluating the effort at all.

"Consistently judging what is good or bad while you are in the moment can be equally distracting."

Consistently judging what is good or bad while you are in the moment can be equally distracting. I'm not saying to be careless. If you sense that you are losing focus, your technique is wavering, or you find yourself considering how awesome you are, by all means, quickly pull yourself back in line. However, resist the urge to have a quality control meeting right then and there.

Think of the everyday scene where the dad is teaching his son to ride a bike. At long last, the wheels start rolling, and the dad yells out, "You're doing it!" Overjoyed with accomplishment while basking in his dad's approval, the boy crashes. He shifts his attention from riding the bike to *what it means* that he is riding the bike. The weight of achievement and the subsequent celebration becomes the focus and a distraction. His limited training and experience in riding a bike cannot withstand the lack of focus. Crash!

I was watching the movie *The Mask* last night, and Jim Carrey's character (Stanley) follows the familiar arc of weak push-over to beautiful-girl-winning, brave hero. As we draw near resolution and the full transformation of wimp to winner, Stanley finds the stones to face the villain (Dorian) in a fight. While Stanley is pounding Dorian's face, he stops, and in somewhat disbelief, says to himself, "I'm winning!" Immediately, Dorian capitalizes on Stanley's distraction and lands a blow. Stanley suddenly loses the advantage.

That, right there, is bona fide proof that positive distraction can be a bad thing! (wink)

In both scenarios above, doubt and insecurity were not the cause of failure. Success was the cause of failure. **The time for evaluating a performance is after the fact.** When performing under any sort of pressure, *just be.* Trust that, at the very least, your Base Level (Hook #4) is good enough. Evaluate later.

THE LAMP REFLECTION

When you can take a few moments and pull away from everything, I want you to try this meditation exercise. Afterward, you should feel more relaxed and in control, but also have a useful analogy for a consistent and composed performance.

1. Find somewhere quiet without any distractions. Sit in a comfortable chair. Calming music or some sort of white noise can be helpful. Avoid music with lyrics. It's hard to meditate while considering the events in "We Didn't Start the Fire," for example. Also, set your music or noise to repeat. Pulling yourself away to reset the tunes defeats the purpose.

2. Close your eyes and slowly take ten comfortable deep breaths. Inhale and exhale through the nose. Each inhale and exhale should last about six seconds. (This breathing exercise alone is useful any time you feel the need to reclaim your thoughts, regain control, and center your emotions. Try it! Hook #51)

3. Allow any and all thoughts without judgment or consideration. Try not to linger on any one thought. My trick—I imagine each thought as a wadded-up piece of paper. One thought after the other is quickly tossed away and out of my mind.

4. After a few moments of relaxed breathing and discarding random thoughts, I want you to imagine a lamp. This lamp can be any shape and size. It can rise from the floor or sit on a table. Is the column flexible or ridged? Is the power switch on the power cord or near the

socket? The light can shine any color, and the bulb can be bare or shaded. Build your lamp. Take your time and consider the details. Imagining this lamp is your only focus and responsibility. Don't rush this process!

5. Now, visualize taking your lamp to the stage, boardroom, conference hall, or wherever you present your honed skills in real life. Find a place to position your lamp. Find a place to plug in your lamp. Turn on the lamp. What do you see? What does this space look like now that your lamp is turned on? Spend as much time here as you would like.

6. Open your eyes.

Beyond the meditation, now consider the symbolism. **You built your lamp to shine. When plugged in, this lamp will function the same way on any table or floor under any circumstance.**

So can be our efforts. Shine on!

HOOK #18

Most successful performances include a triumphant recovery.

I NEED ANGELA Lansbury to sing the following line: "Tale as old as time."

All of our heroes go through some sort of peril. They are confronted with an obstacle, burden, or challenge that appears to be insurmountable. Typically, when despair seems to be the only option and defeat is all but certain, the hero finds something deep within and restores order through victory.

Would we even know of the phoenix without the ashes whence it rises? Who is Rocky but your average no-name boxer without Apollo Creed, Clubber Lang, Drago, and yes, Thunderlips? Frank Sinatra, at one point, transformed from superstar to washed-up has-been. Personal issues, a shift in the public's musical taste, and his inability to perform at his established level spelled doom for the greatest vocalist in American pop history. Yet, his most defining years were still ahead of him. Frank's second act defined his career and established what we now recognize as the Great American Songbook.

These stories are endless and, yes, as old as time. The rescue. The reinvention. The resuscitation. The recovery. The resurrection.

Let's go back to Rocky. He's a poor, humble boxer. He's the underdog preparing to face the champion. His journey is one of personal pain and uncertainty. Yet, he perseveres, claiming one incremental victory at a time. He wins the heart of Adrian. He convinces Mick that he has the stomach to train. He catches the chicken! And in the most moving scene in movie history, he stands by Adrian's side, waiting for her to come out of the coma. Neglecting his selfish needs to train and his desire to take on Apollo Creed, he remains bedside with his ailing wife. Then, supported by the low thunder of the string and the clang of the bell, Adrian awakens from her deep sleep and intently encourages her husband to WIN!

The championship fight becomes a micro representation of Rocky's life story. The ebb and flow of both boxers landing critical blows. Each trading the upper hand yet still facing the long fight. The cuts and swelling. Fatigue and blood. The falling and stumbling. The apprehension that our hero had finally met his match. The extreme suffering that causes even Adrian to look away.

Yet, as we all know, Rocky prevails. He wins. He becomes the champion. He makes enough money to buy a robot (a 1983 robot, mind you).

Understand that struggle is part of success. You cannot avoid uncertainty, doubt, and fear. It's real in life and performance. It will affect you.

However, there is no shame in feeling these emotions. There is no shame in being affected by these emotions. We all must learn to recover. To press on. To understand that, most likely, our audience will not see nor hear our errors, and even if they do, it's ok. They will forgive us for being human. Let that bad note pass on by and sing the next one better. Forget that you stumbled through the opening joke to no laughter. Move right to the heart of the matter. Win them over with your purpose.

"Allow your message and song to rise above your imperfections and wobbles. Win them over with your purpose."

Do not be surprised when punched in the mouth. Expect it and hit back. Allow your message and song to rise above your imperfections and wobbles.

When I struggle in a performance, I do not suffer by ruminating over my mistakes after making a recovery. I've learned I will, more than likely, get in my way with wandering thoughts of doubt, anxiety, and insecurity. Rather than aim to entirely rid me of these thoughts (Don't think about an elephant right now! You just did, didn't you?), I accept them as flashes. Flash and move on, feeling no shame. Sometimes, I have to endure the burn of the flash. Yet, when the heat cools, I am bolstered by my ability to have taken the heat, remained engaged, and committed to my endeavor. I've removed the emotion of surprise. I will not be blindsided. There will be a punch. There will be a flash. There will be heat. Even so, I will withstand and recover. Yo, Adrian! I will triumph!

THE WASH TECHNIQUE

I made one of those things! You know, an acronym. I think it's helpful. Remember the Base Level theory, and the water, and the flooding (Hook #4)? Well, when you can feel the water's approaching and the pressure is mounting, don't get flooded, just let it WASH away.

- **W**elcome the adversity in whatever form it manifests (fear and doubt are the big ones, usually). Don't be surprised. Don't fight it. Expect it. You are human; these things happen.

- **A**ccept the discomfort. Getting upset that your palms are sweaty, thoughts are racing, and breath is short makes things worse. These reactions will pass.

- **S**tay on task. Continue to do what you have trained to do. Don't bail out! Remember, picturing something that gives you joy can divert your attention just enough so that you can get out of your own way (Hook #5). Breathe deeply through the nose.

- **H**arness the confidence and pride that follows overcoming adversity. Channel that resilience into poise, which is defined as a stably balanced state. Pretty cool, right!

CONFIDENCE

How to gain, accept, and retain confidence

HOOK #19

"Confidence comes from demonstrated ability."

– Bill Parcells

I'M A HUGE football fan. I enjoy watching and reading about the sport.

When asked about a player's confidence level, the great football coach Bill Parcells said, "Confidence comes from demonstrated ability." Awesome! Throughout my career, that line has remained impactful.

"I allow myself the reward of confidence."

Like many performers, I have struggled with insecurity and anxiety. I have applied this quote in two ways:

1. I understand that for me to be confident in a certain task, I need to demonstrate that I can do it consistently at the desired level.

2. Once I demonstrate that ability, I allow myself the reward of confidence.

Often, performers will continue to struggle with performance issues even after they have demonstrated, countless times, that they can perform at an acceptable level.

Work on a skill until you can perform it with consistency, and then accept the confidence that comes from that hard work.

HOOK #20

Don't focus so much on your shortcomings that you rob yourself of the chance to gain confidence from your strengths.

AS OLIVIA NEWTON-JOHN once sang, "Let's get technical, technical."

The term cognitive distortion refers to faulty or inaccurate thinking, perception, or belief. Really smart people have determined that many of us are susceptible to a handful of cognitive distortions. (There's a compiled list of these. Very insightful! I recommend taking a look.)

One of those distortions is all or nothing thinking. The common psychological acronym for this distortion is ANTS, which stands for Automatic Negative Thoughts. In this case, I prefer my acronym: ANTS—All or Nothing Thoughts. (Can you copyright an acronym? I promise, I didn't know there was already an ANTS acronym when I wrote this. For a minute I thought I was a genius and really onto something. Oh well!)

Anyway, ANTS crawl around your brain and leave zero room for error. Everything is black and white. One small step short of perfection and the whole thing is a failure! It's either ALL GOOD or ALL BAD.

I suspect that anyone who performs or offers some sort of presentation suffers from the infestation of ANTS a little or a lot. I know I did and sometimes still do.

As a young man with little experience on a national stage, I struggled with consistency while in *Movin' Out*. As I've stated before, my biggest challenge with the show wasn't my talent, but my ability to deliver the same level of performance every show. That was the gig. Do it the same, all the time. I couldn't.

Those pesky ANTS held me back. At the end of each show, I would obsess over a few wrong notes here and there, or sections where I felt uncertain and anxious. The show was almost two hours long, and I was only focused on my failures and errors. This led to frustration, fretting, insecurity, and fear.

The healthy and most productive thinking would have been something along the lines of, "Matt, sure you made some mistakes, but you were also spot-on for most of the show. Accept that the ability you demonstrated for the majority of the show can give you the confidence to perform at a consistently high level and also correct your mistakes." Rather than wallowing in the ANT pile, I should have gravitated to the fact that I was an awesome rock star, fronting a million-dollar show.

There's a saying: "Aim for perfection and achieve excellence." The point is, perfection is almost impossible to achieve, but excellence is attainable. The fact that perfection is practically impossible inherently suggests that there will be errors.

For growth, you must recognize your failures, learn how to correct them, and take action. It's also imperative to reward yourself for your abilities and successes. When it comes to a perspective, all or nothing thinking is a choice. Accept that there can be both good and bad concurrently.

I would argue that a life well lived is balanced between taking familiar paths for comfort and losing your way on roads less traveled. It's ok to be lost for a while, to be wrong, to make errors. Of course, it's also ok to feel confident in your direction, be right, and to achieve. Allow yourself to be both.

Irrational, bad, untruthful, negative, unforgiving, and fearful thoughts will clutter your mind and fester like rotting trash. Rotting trash attracts ANTS.

Empty your trash, dude!

HOOK #21

Draw confidence from what sets you apart.

THROUGHOUT MY CAREER, it became evident that my best performances included stories and banter in between songs. Although I was having success in "songs only" shows, the format limited my opportunity to communicate, and the shows were not as good. Over time, I identified my strengths, and now I consider myself an entertainer first and foremost—not just a musician.

It's rewarding to know that you are really good at something. You can find a way to channel that realization to other areas of your performance. I use my ability to sing, play the piano, write, and perform songs to share my message and entertain. My confidence comes from having embraced the fact that I'm a great entertainer.

During any show, I have learned to identify when I am losing focus and allowing thoughts like, "What do I sound like?" "Do these people like me?" "Can I hit that note today?" I immediately pull myself back into the moment and draw confidence from my lifelong experience of being good at what I do.

I have learned to use the confidence I've earned from my strengths to inspire the belief that I can overcome my limitations. By choosing not to give in to the doubt and focusing on what sets me apart, I'm more apt to perform to the best of my ability.

If you put the work into getting better at something, sometimes the only thing preventing you from success is doubt. And doubt doesn't have to be real.

That's cool, right?

Jump to Hook #48 to read more on this topic.

HOOK #22

*A pleasant sound in private
has the potential to be
a pleasant sound in public.*

THERE'S A RULE old-school coaches live by: "If they did it once, they can do it again." In other words, if we've seen Jim kick it sixty yards, then we know he can kick it sixty yards.

The first step to honing a skill is getting it right in the practice room. (Again, the old adage, "Don't practice until you get it right. Practice until you can't get it wrong. Then it's right!")

Of course, performing something in public brings added pressure compared to practicing a skill in private.

Keep the faith! When alone, if you have heard the sweet sounds of your voice (a pleasant sound), or seen the elegant moves of your dance, or made it through two pages of memorized dialogue uninterrupted, then believe you can do it for others.

Realize there are different skills in play here. One is the physical movement to talk, sing, play, dance, hit, shoot, or whatever the desired skillset may be. The other skill is the mental ability to focus and allow your body to perform in stressful situations.

Have hope that if you can learn one skill, you can learn another.

Performing in public is not a mystery. It doesn't require your audience to be naked either!

HOOK #23

Choosing a task without the skills to complete it may lead to criticism and loss of confidence.

I FIND IT interesting that overconfidence can quickly lead to a lack of confidence. Rather than returning to a clear head that is aware and in control, we are prone to move on directly to hesitation and doubt.

My boys do this all the time. They venture too high on the monkey bars or climb too far out on the tree limb because their inexperience and over-confidence are dominant. Once they perceive they are in trouble, they call "Daddy!" when, most times, they could easily take the same steps back to their comfort zone. Furthermore, once rescued, they identify the monkey bars or tree limb as dangerous, and something they don't want any part of moving forward.

Sometimes, I'll find myself "climbing too far out on the limb" during a performance. I'm relaxed and confident. I feel completely in control of my body, and perceive I'm sounding good. Next thing I know, I'm trying out new material. Material that should be rehearsed, but "Who cares that I've never played this song; I'm very awesome right now! Let's do it anyway." Now and then I get away with this bravado. However, more often than not, I start to hear my inexperience with the song. Certain passages are more difficult without practice. Some parts of the tune I just don't know. I become self-conscious, like all performers do when they are struggling onstage. My body starts to react as if I'm really in a mess. (FYI, it never fails that this is the exact moment someone decides to take out their phone and shoot video!)

"...overconfidence can quickly lead to a lack of confidence."

Through experience, I've learned how to retrace my steps and crawl back on that limb to where there is a healthy level of confidence. Whereas before, my adventurous spirit put me in an uncomfortable state that left me out there tentative, searching, and insecure.

I would never encourage anyone to live life cautiously or perform hesitantly. We all need to channel our inner stuntman. Yet, stuntmen are aware of what they are doing beforehand. They have prepared and use their expertise to manipulate their body and surroundings. The risks they take are bold yet calculated, not haphazard. While a wrong move can injure the stuntman, a poor choice from a performer can leave lasting traces of doubt and insecurity, unwarranted and preventable.

Again, professional performance is rooted in physical skill and mental focus. Presenting something to your audience that is beyond your skill level can certainly fuddle the latter.

That's fun to say, "fuddle the latter." Change it to "ladder," and you have a saying: "Don't fuddle the ladder!" Building confidence is like climbing a ladder of experience. Don't fuddle the ladder. You get it?

If you do decide to take a risk, keep the results in perspective. Shrug off the mistakes.

Lest you want a fuddled ladder. Ok, I'm done.

HOOK #24

Take your warm-up swing far away from the ball.

MY DAD USED to say this, and it always made me laugh. Think about it. The golfer approaches his ball on the tee, takes a practice swing, and accidentally hits the ball. He has an entire golf course to find a place to practice a swing that doesn't have to be anywhere near the ball. Yet, he gets so close to the ball to take a swing (that he knows won't count), and then he hits the ball unintentionally. Dumb!

I continually tell one of my artists to "only accept opportunities when you are confident that you can deliver the product." I remind him that it's ok to say no if he is not prepared. When needed, he should invest the time to get better before accepting an offer. Once he's taken the offer, he will be judged by the results. Fair or not, first impressions are crucial (Hook #69).

I recall meeting an influential member of Billy Joel's band in a social setting. Auditions for *Movin' Out* had not begun, so I was not involved professionally in any way. Things were relaxed, and we started talking about Billy Joel tunes, playing the piano, performing, and my career. He mentioned they were looking for piano players for the show and asked if I would like to play for him, right then and there. Not fully considering the situation, I eagerly said yes. After a few minutes of showcasing my ability to play the songs *sorta kinda*, he said, "You don't know the chords." Again, this guy played in Billy's band. He KNEW the tunes. My approximation of the songs was not too impressive, and the impromptu jam ended abruptly. I made an impression all right. A bad one! I took a practice swing and hit the ball.

Of course, things worked out in the end. However, my "practice swing" could have cost me.

Be aware and be prepared. Approach "the ball" only when you are ready to hit and take your turn.

SKILL

Getting better at what you do

HOOK #25

One of the first steps to honing a craft is to recognize "what it's NOT."

AS I HAVE made clear throughout our time together, I did not study music in school.

Early in my career, I would routinely rely on mentors and peers for guidance and quality control. I didn't trust my ear to identify errors and inconsistencies.

I'm amused when I recall my approach to my craft as a young man. Rather than understanding that at the very base of each composition were individual notes arranged together to make a song, I just listened to the song overall. Until I learned what a bass line should sound like, or how to pluck out a melody on the piano to match what I wanted to sing, I had to rely on others to tell me right from wrong.

Throughout my first decade of making records, I insisted on using the same producer because I knew he wouldn't let wrong notes slip by. I didn't trust my ability to manage that task.

Hearing music can appear to be some sort of voodoo magic to the untrained. I know that over time, I began to at least *hear* what wasn't right. Although I wasn't always sure what to do about it, I accepted the criticism and critique. I welcomed being wrong because I wanted the project to be successful. I paid attention to what needed to be corrected and why.

Musically, learning the magic of *hearing* allowed me to identify the flaws and make corrections. Whereas before, I was throwing musical darts at a target without aiming true.

Unattended, my little boy will put his shirt on backward and his shoes on the wrong feet. I taught him that the shirt pocket goes in the front. Now he knows when it's not right. How does he know? Because I told him. He understands that if the pocket is not on the front of the shirt, he is wearing it incorrectly. He's got it down, mostly. (Some shirts don't have pockets.)

As far as the shoes, he asks me every time, "Daddy, is this the right foot?" Why does he ask? Because he is now aware that each shoe goes on a particular foot. There was a time in his life when he was oblivious to this reality. Currently, he may not know how to manage this task alone, but he's progressed to the stage of understanding that there is a right way for the shoe to fit. One day soon, I will pretend not to hear him ask which shoe goes on the proper foot. I want him to feel what it is and what it's not. From there, he will learn the magic of putting on a shoe.

By the way, it *is* quite magical to little Harry! His ability to conquer the shirt and shoe is an extraordinary power he is aiming to master.

I believe we learn more from "what it's not" than from "what it is." We all know this as "trial and error." The first step, however, is to realize that there even is a "what it's not" and then how to identify it!

Trust those around you that know more. Follow their instruction. Listen when they offer critique. Seek out the errors!

Learn the magic.

Otherwise, you may go through life wearing backward clothes, uncomfortable shoes, and singing out of tune.

HOOK #26

*Your best effort
will come from knowing
your current state of skill.*

WE ALL CARRY a perception of who we are professionally and personally. This perception shapes our confidence and determines our performance level. For instance, consider the late-night talk show where a professional athlete squares off against the host in a silly contest (like David Letterman and quarterback Peyton Manning throwing footballs into taxicab windows).

The host will always say something like, "Here goes nothing!" or "I'm probably not good at this, but I'll try anyway." Deservedly, they may not be that good at the challenge. However, they eliminate almost any chance for success by resigning to the notion that they are "probably not good at this." (I know! The point of the bit is not to win but to entertain. The entertainment value can be high whether or not the host makes the throw. However, it's always better when they "make the throw.")

In any case, the big point here is that low expectations allow room for low effort and acceptance of failure.

In turn, overconfidence and a distorted perception of one's ability can set a path to undesired consequences. The saying, "Hold my beer!" has become a catchphrase that has made its way into the cultural lexicon. It merely implies, "Watch me do something more stupid than that other guy while I project extreme confidence and zero self-awareness." (For example, just search YouTube for someone trying to jump off their roof into a swimming pool on a tricycle or a guy hitting a golf ball with a canoe paddle on fire.)

All in all, an accurate and honest gauge of one's ability is necessary for performing any task at a high level.

Your ability will change over time. If you are honing your craft, you will most likely get better. Accept the rewards of your efforts and gain more confidence. Or recognize when you need to sharpen your skills. If you are not paying attention, those skills you used to be good at will diminish. You might confidently attempt something that you are no longer proficient at due to neglect.

"If you are not paying attention, those skills you used to be good at will diminish."

Studies prove that just getting older will contribute to a decline in ability and performance. Although there are cognitive compensations and flat out, God-given abilities one can rely on, in truth, the only way to maintain peak performance in a field is to maintain a purposeful practice routine. Maintaining that skill through practice is required. Otherwise, your skill will decline.

Learning how to practice is an entirely separate skill from performing.

Within your craft, find techniques and routines that target your weaknesses and strengthen your fundamentals. Practice these methods until they become habit or second nature. Then, follow a practice regimen that helps you maintain your Base Level (Hook #4) and supports continued improvement.

Onstage results will follow.

HOOK #27

Inspired work pays off!

BEFORE LEAVING *MOVIN'* *Out,* the musical director sat down with me to discuss an overview of my time with the show. Part of that discussion addressed my strengths and weaknesses. Kindly, he advised that I work on my vocal consistency. I was already aware of this limitation and its role in possibly preventing me from reaching even greater heights in my career. I wanted and needed to get better. I just didn't know how.

So, with time on my hands and the freedom to experiment, I became obsessed with learning every trick and technique available. I learned the principles of speech level singing. I studied the fundamentals of traditional vocal techniques (breathing, placement, vowel shapes, etc.). I practiced ear training and sang into a digital tuner to *see* where I was sharp or flat. (Mostly flat. Ugh!) I studied varied opinions on posture for an optimal vocal while standing and while sitting at the piano. I invested in lessons and books. I scoured the internet for videos and articles. I identified and sought counsel from peers who were trained and more experienced. I would practice in my car while driving. I would practice while walking down the street or exercising. I was determined to become a better singer.

At any point since then, I could have given up and accepted my limitations. However, I chose to get better. My desire to get better was inspired and still is today. I'm a far better singer now than when I left the tour years ago.

What does inspired work look like?

1. Identify your weakness.

2. Tap into a motivator for inspiration. For example, I'm competitive and want to win. I view poor performances as "losing." A bad performance makes me want to work harder to be better. Other motivators could be money, recognition, status, sense of accomplishment, pride in your work, etc.

3. Use this inspiration to learn how to get better and go to work. (Getting better is a skill. Hook #26)

HOOK #28

Muscle memory is powerful.
Use it for your benefit,
not your detriment.

WE'VE DISCUSSED THE impact muscle memory has on training and getting better at your craft. It is a key and undeniable factor related to any function that requires physical skill and effort. Of course, it makes sense to formulate a plan or practice regimen that strengthens and trains positive muscle memory. When a person goes to the gym, they typically have a sense of their motivation in mind: "I'm going to lose weight," or "I'm going to get bigger and stronger," or "It's January, and I paid for this so I might as well go." We all understand and are aware of this line of reasoning.

What we often disregard is what happens when we ignore muscle memory. Truthfully, we are contributing to our muscle memory, whether we are intending to or not. If I continue to sing unknowingly with a tight jaw and tense neck, I will more than likely always sing that way. In turn, I will always struggle. I'm telling my muscles, "This is ok," and "Let's add another layer of memory to this constriction." I've seen it too many times where the hobbyist musician sits in with the band and screws up. Afterward, there is a sense of embarrassment and disappointment. They wonder why they didn't perform better. It's quite simple. Unknowingly, they have trained their body to perform poorly by not actively training to perform successfully. The quote about insanity, often misattributed to Einstein, might be appropriate here: "The definition of insanity is doing the same thing over and over again and expecting a different result."

A teacher once told me to observe the perfect posture of my one-year-old boy. His shoulders were relaxed, his neck was long and straight, and his back was flat and stable. My little boy hadn't been affected by years of stress and strain. Our bodies are designed to work for us, but circumstances (some out of our control) and habits begin to wear down that efficiency over time.

Every moment offers an opportunity to carry our body correctly and in the way it was intended. Doing so, you can relieve tension while increasing function. Not doing so produces the opposite.

It's going to go one way or the other. Why not choose the better way?

IDENTITY & EXPECTATIONS

Thoughts for the professional and personal you

HOOK #29

Plan for the future.
Don't live in it.

WHERE DID THE time go?

When I was in my mid-twenties, I was fortunate to have a full-time, well-paying gig on Austin's famed Sixth Street. Five nights a week (or more), I would hold court behind the piano at the renowned Ivory Cat Tavern. Locals and visitors from all over the world would gather round the edge of my stage, or in the bleachers that lined the back wall, to raise a glass and sing until they ran out of throat. These were some of the best days of my life.

On any given night, however, one would be hard-pressed to determine if the real excitement was in the Tavern or out on the street. The Sixth Street legend was more than just a row of establishments or local musicians that graced the dimly lit stages. The eclectic group of people that walked among us nightly shared the blame here too. Texas State Senators, University of Texas Greeks, movie stars, rock stars (bona fide or imagined), food vendors, jewelry vendors, junk vendors, cross-dressers, no-dressers (nekkid, as we say in Texas), folks on convention (the wildest, mind you), folks on vacation, and good ol' plain Austinites, just to name a few, marched up and down the stone sidewalks. As I said, these were some of the best days of my life.

Although slightly frowned upon by the owner, I took one break a night. Never at midnight, because people would say, "Well, it's midnight, so let's go home." Never too close to midnight, because people would say, "Well, it's *close* to midnight, so let's go home." Never at 11:30 because we started at 9:00, and that's too soon to take a break. 12:15, maybe? 12:30 was usually the sweet spot. On this one now memorable night, I strolled out to the street just a few minutes after leaving the stage. I had just a few moments (fifteen moments to be exact) to enjoy my break, so I figured I would leave the haze and get some fresh air. Stationed within the regular cast of characters, I noticed a man and woman holding a big burlap sack that drew a considerable amount of attention. Curious, I sauntered over, as young rock stars do, and looked in the bag.

Puppies!

I reached into the bag and grabbed a fur ball. As I turned its little face toward mine, I was unaware that I was about to be overwhelmed. The only thing I can say is that I instantly loved little Belle at that moment. I remember saying, "How much?" I had the fifty dollars in cash they were asking, and the deal was done. Still, with a set to go, I put little Ladybug (she has a lot of names, ok!) in the breakroom and said, "I'll be right back."

Bug was my little girl for quite a long time. There was an era when, if you knew Matt, then you knew Laybug (still more names). She was kind of my own Forrest Gump. Pick a major event in my life, and she's been around in some way. Girlfriends, gigs, tours, marriage, kids, first house—you get the point.

I recall lying in bed and bawling my eyes out the night before she was to turn ten years old. We all know that dogs don't live forever, and ten seemed like an ominous milestone. I was afraid the best dog in the world was near the end, just because she was about to turn ten.

Belle was the ruler of the house and would communicate as if she was aware of her standing. We would joke that when she wanted back inside from relieving herself or sniffing the air, there was no ramp-up to the "let me in." Her first bark was as if she had been waiting for hours. And, she never slept outside! Never!

The night before she died, she slept out on the back porch, underneath the moon and the stars. She was eighteen years old.

Where did the time go?

I'm not sure that I can add too much more to the discussion on mindfulness and living in the moment. So much has already been said, and I would only be repeating. Yet, the tears in my eyes right now, as I recall my sweet Belle and the night younger me pulled her out of that brown sack, remind me that time is precious, and we need to relish what we get.

Having goals, plans, and ideas for life and work are essential. However, many times, we get caught up in the excitement, wonder, and even anxiety about the future that we pay little attention to the present.

Ten years can become eighteen in the blink of an eye. Don't miss out while planning for the future.

HOOK #30

*You are not as good
as you think you are.
And, you are not as bad
as they say you are.*

I OFFER ANOTHER lesson passed on from my friend and mentor, Ray McGee. As mentioned before, Ray was my first true musical mentor. We became stage partners in the dueling piano show at Disney, and my time working with Ray left an indelible mark on my career.

Back to the Hook. **Make sure your first opinion of yourself is your own. Be truthful and knowledgeable in your assessment.**

"You must develop discernment when it comes to criticism."

Without caution, we can develop exaggerated opinions of our abilities. Often, this self-admiration suppresses the desire to learn and improve. Similarly, other's opinions *can* matter and be valid. Though, people's opinions are, at times, selfishly motivated. You must develop discernment when it comes to criticism.

If what they are saying is true, make it better. If what they are saying is false, move on. (More on this in Hook #66.)

HOOK #31

Apply the Base Level concept to your personal life.

IF IT'S TRUE that we can have a Base Level of performance (Hook #4), then we can also have a Base Level in our behavior and reactions. There is a Base Level to our anger, our enthusiasm, our acceptance of others, our intolerance, our kindness, and even our love.

I became aware that I had zero tolerance when talking to a customer service agent on the phone. More often than not, the call was in response to a problem with a product or service. Typically, the very nature of the call was confrontational. I found no matter how calm I promised to remain, my frustration would always rise in the end.

Eventually, I realized these stressful interactions were attitude altering and left a murky residue on my day. My mood would turn sour. I'd feel shame for allowing my emotions to appear out of control.

I made the decision to do better. I made the decision to work on this frustration. I decided to turn my irritation into a calmer exchange with the customer service agent while remaining in control and cordial.

By merely recognizing the toll these interactions were taking on my emotions, and by aiming to handle the frustration in a better way, I raised the Base Level of my intolerance and anger. No matter how inept the customer service agent was at his job, I was determined to stay focused and be cool. His murky water was not going to erode my higher ground!

So there I was, once again, discussing a matter with my nemesis, the "customer service agent." I could feel my frustration level was high. Inwardly, I became intolerant and impatient. I "bit my tongue" and restrained myself from interrupting the robotic, disengaged, and illogical "reasoning" I was being offered. I responded calmly and directly while controlling what used to be my typical reaction. My issue was resolved, and I walked away mood intact. By applying the Base Level concept, I raised my ability to manage my frustration and resist the urge to "give 'em the ol' what for!"

Whereas before, my Base Level was quick to anger and frustration; now, my Base Level is controlled and composed. (I'm still working on it!)

Throughout all of my life, I find instances where raising my Base Level would be a benefit. Interactions with my wife and children. Interactions with my family, my mother, and my father. Interactions with my peers and associates. I can always do better and create a Base Level that is controlled, harmonious, and loving, rather than unfiltered and reactionary.

One could argue that our Base Level reactions are habits or reflexes. Habits can be changed. Reflexes can be unlearned and reprogrammed.

Consider your Base Level reactions and interactions in your daily life. Do you see recurring instances where you could be calmer and more tolerant? At times do you think, *Man, I could have handled that better!?*

Identify these moments and reactions and then create an environment that reminds you of your desire to change. For example, I set notifications on my phone that pop up throughout the day that read *Be Cool* or *Be Patient.* They are little reminders to keep my emotions in check and not let life's small irritants get the better of me.

Identifying where you want a higher Base Level, learning how to manage your reactions, and then implementing a system that reminds you to do so is the magic here.

Try it, it really works!

HOOK #32

Behavior you tolerate from others is how they will respond.

I CAN THINK of three instances where I purposely valued someone's talent and contribution to my project over their reliability and professionalism.

I'll refer to them as "members" here since they were members of the band. Member one was consistently late, forgetful, made excuses, and at times, untrustworthy. Member two was irreverent, socially intrusive, and ignored the band's agreed-upon rules. Member three had issues that caused several problems, professionally and personally.

Yet, member one was a genius who could solve any technical issue and brought cutting-edge creativity to the band's sound and presentation. Member two was a brilliant musician who could hear and direct arrangements while also playing the most appropriate style and feel on any song. Member three was integral to the band's sound and finding a replacement would've been a major step backward, a step taken without the promise of the band ever sounding the same again.

While working with these band members, I tried every way possible to change their professional behavior. One-on-one talks, heated confrontations, and reviewing performance expectations were just some of the strategies attempted. Although these efforts sometimes prompted minor adjustments, overall, things remained the same. Eventually, I realized that by maintaining their employment, I was tolerating their actions. No amount of talking was going to change their behavior. At this point, it was my problem, not theirs (Hook #44).

Ultimately, we moved on from relying on these members regularly.

"I prefer to share my expectations with those close to me and then look for common ground to bring about my requests."

Take the good with the bad or find someone else. In the end, I chose to find someone else. The band was happier and easier to manage. And, we found a different but similar sound that was free from the frustration and stress.

Here's a quick observation about personal relationships: When it comes to friends and family, we are more likely committed to solving our issues rather than "firing" someone because they have annoying or unpleasing behavior. I prefer to share my expectations with those close to me and then look for common ground to bring about my requests. I insist I receive treatment grounded in respect, love, and fairness. I am careful to make sure I am offering the same in return.

What you tolerate is what you get!

HOOK #33

Give someone as many chances as you can tolerate.

AFTER A SUCCESSFUL solo career, Don Henley once said that returning to the Eagles brought on a sense of relief, and he welcomed the shared responsibility being in a band allowed (I am paraphrasing here). As a solo artist, he carried the burden all alone.

Leading any band or team requires managing relationships, personalities, behaviors, motivations, and logistics. It's easy to become annoyed by even the smallest of things. As a bandleader, I have to continually regulate my emotions and remind myself that minor variances to the process are just that—minor.

Sure, someone is always fifteen minutes late to load in, won't return calls in a timely fashion, or insist on making inconvenient food requests. The constant bombardment of these minor nuisances will add up. However, if the band's overall performance and reputation remain intact and there's a sense of camaraderie, it's prudent to endure the "paper cuts."

As a leader, you will lose credibility and voice with your team if you are constantly nagging and correcting. You will find that these small and consistent annoyances are not that big a deal, overall. When it finally comes to the point that you cannot tolerate a team member or behavior any longer, then address the situation.

Removing a member of a band or team can be destructive and time-consuming. Before making a change, you must weigh the time commitment required to bring in somebody new verses the struggle of managing the difficult member. Be patient.

Yes, I believe the behavior you tolerate from others is how they will respond (Hook #32). However, ask yourself if you are just on edge and if things are really that bad before you take action.

Encourage positive behavior by complimenting the good, rather than correcting the bad. When you just can't stand someone's actions any longer, make a change.

HOOK #34

Performers will always assume it's about them.
It's not.

I'VE STRUGGLED WITH this assumption my entire career. Art (music, writing, acting) is probably the most personal professional medium. Anything created by experience, presented as a product, and most often performed or delivered by the artist, is personal *to that artist.* An artist's success is often equated to a creative idea (song, book, play) that garners public adulation or a memorable and rewarding performance showered with praise. When an artist steps under the lights or presents a soul-baring performance for public approval, there is a risk. Rejection, apathy, and even ridicule lie waiting to pounce. Mind you, that rejection is not in the lines of, "Hey Michelin, I don't like those tires," or "Hey Target, I don't like those bath towels." **With any form of rejection, the artist hears, "I don't like you!"**

Having said that, this assumption by the performer can be unfounded. In a perfect environment, an artist presents his or her work in a space without distraction to an attentive and eager audience. A performance on point should yield a satisfied crowd. Unfortunately, the perfect environment is rarely available to the average working artist. Musicians play venues and events where the music is for ambiance, not attention. Actors grab on to whatever work they can find, even if that means in substandard theaters with little support. Painters hang their art in restaurants for exposure, yet in the end, lose out to the artichoke dip.

Consider all factors when grading your performance.

Give your absolute best at all times. Take responsibility for reaching your audience. Be prepared to adjust your strategy if necessary. Comply with the venue's or client's requests. If that garners a successful show and rave reviews, then celebrate that the circumstances worked in your favor. If you did your best to little or no fanfare, understand there might have been a football game on in the bar, or the guests at the fundraiser were too busy socializing, or the guy in the front row never dances—ever!

We can also apply this idea to sales. Your product and pitch might be precisely what someone needs and wants, just not at the moment. So often, we send out an email or make a call with a proposal, and we wait. As a few days go by, the natural doubts begin to creep in: "They didn't like my pitch," or "They don't want to buy." Maybe so. Yet, it's possible they just haven't made time to review your offer. Remember, your career revolves around what you are selling and promoting. Their career does not. An evasive response, or no response at all, does not necessarily mean rejection. (Even if it does mean rejection now, that certainly does not close the door on future opportunities.)

I'm working with a guy right now who has been pitching his services to me for over a decade. His presentations and services were always appealing. However, my business needs and budgets did not line up with his offering and expertise—until now. From his perspective, ten years is a long time to wait for *that* email! HA! (I bet you currently have important unread emails in your inbox right now. You will get to them when the time is right for you. Right? See, it goes both ways! Why are you causing those people so much stress? Set this book down and go reply to some emails!)

When I was a kid, I would go to camp every summer. During orientation, the counselors would say, "You will have a great time this week if you expect to." **Expectations affect participation and response.** Everyone expects to have a great time going to see Beyoncé or Paul McCartney. Not everyone expects to have a great time seeing Matt Wilson. In fact, they may have no expectations at all. Why? *'Cause I'm not super famous like Beyoncé or Paul McCartney.* Very few are! The rest of us must perform and present our artistry or message in all kinds of environments and hope to connect with an audience with expectations of being entertained, informed, sold, or enlightened.

A disappointing result does not necessarily mean a bad performance or pitch. Learn to differentiate between a bad show and a distracted audience.

You may be making unneeded changes to your product based on a preoccupied public.

The famous breakup line might work here in reverse: "It's not me; it's you!" (More to consider on this topic in Hook #13.)

HOOK #35

"Who I think I am" and "Who I am" may not be the same. Learn to evaluate yourself objectively.

THROUGHOUT THIS BOOK, I will continue to share my journey of self-evaluation as a man and as a performer. In this case, I want to share an experience from another performer's perspective.

Routinely, I book "all-request, sing-along" piano bars. These shows consist of a piano player and a drummer taking requests from the audience and encouraging interaction through singing along and dancing. One of the most challenging aspects of the gig is keeping up with the vast amount of material the audience draws on for requests. Many of the old-guard piano bar players are resistant to learning modern tunes for one reason or another. These seasoned players, who were once the gold standard, now find themselves ineffective in their efforts.

I recall one difficult conversation with a local piano bar legend who simply couldn't do the gig any longer because his delivery and material were not current. His first reaction was to remind me of his accomplishments and who he was professionally. I agreed, but I had to point out that he wasn't that any longer in this format. Without putting in the work to remain current, he was mainly a tribute to the past. Although we never spoke in detail about the matter, I believe he called a "meeting of one" and determined that this style of entertainment no longer suited him. He was one of the best, and now he wasn't. The good news is that he went on to find a very lucrative and rewarding gig that fit the "new" him.

Critical self-evaluation is imperative. It's a good way to remain employed, and while you're at it, enjoy your work.

HOOK #36

Forecast the need for change and reinvention.

I AM WRITING this on a brisk January morning. The brand of the new year has slightly faded, and we are all now focusing on this year's efforts. As one is prone to do, I am mentally taking stock of my current responsibilities and future plans. Age, marriage, and fatherhood have changed me drastically. I am no longer the man who wore this skin ten years ago. Nor do I have the same ambitions, goals, and desires of that younger me.

Some of the change, professionally, can be attributed to the evolution of my industry. It's no secret that the business of music has experienced a drastic transformation over the past thirty years. Without sharing the details here, I'll just say that I see a need for reinvention. My career path up to this point is no longer sustainable nor as desirable to me moving forward. Even if I were to ignore the *desire* part of the equation, there are market considerations (age, ability, competition, proximity, product value, product distribution, product availability, etc.) that have altered the "sky's the limit" promise of my twenty-one-year-old self's starting projections.

By no means am I giving up! However, I am quite mindful that my dreams, goals, and desires from, say, 2005 have changed. They have changed within me, and the path to achieve those goals has become cluttered by those conditions mentioned previously.

There is a joke among some musicians that goes as follows: "If you want to identify in what period a musician was most successful, look at his hairstyle." Musicians will hold on to that mullet, buzz cut, or Flock of Seagulls *do*, current fashion be dammed! If it worked in 1984, it's gonna work again!

Know when it's time to get a haircut—times change.

HOOK #37

Knowing that you have a choice can be more important than the choice you make.

MY FAMILY CAME to visit me when I was a semi-new resident of New Orleans. They had never been to New Orleans, so we wanted to hit as many of the traditional tourist highlights as possible. With seven young children and two grandparents in tow, we moved kind of slowly and with chaos. One of the many to-do ideas batted around was to ride the downtown trolley. I was new to the city and rarely in a place to need the trolley. So, I had little to no knowledge of the process. Where does it go? Where do you get on? How much does it cost? These are all relatively simple questions that could be answered with just a little bit of research— research I had yet to take on.

At any rate, we didn't ride the trolley. (Actually, they are called streetcars in New Orleans. For this story, I'll continue to call them trolleys because that's what I thought they were called at the time.) However, we did go to the Audubon Zoo (among many things we did that week). On the last day of the visit, as we walked through the French Quarter on Decatur Street (between Jackson Square and the Mississippi River), I noticed a trolley parked on the tracks. The sign said, "Audubon Zoo." Who knew! I was slightly disappointed we didn't take the trolley to the zoo, *and* we didn't know that we had the option. Who knows whether the trolley stop would have been convenient for our gang? I didn't (and still don't). The point is, I wasn't aware I had a choice to begin with. I wasn't aware of my choice.

From the mildly inconsequential (You mean, I didn't have to get fries as my side?) to the life-changing (I can make decisions about my life, and I'm not a victim of my circumstances), **people encounter not knowing they have a choice every day.**

In almost every aspect of my life, I'm always asking, "Do I have a choice?" When the answer is clearly yes, then I weigh my options. When faced with a perceived unwanted, inevitable, or undeniable circumstance, I look for a way out before resigning to the outcome.

Just because you don't *feel* like you have a choice, doesn't mean one doesn't exist.

It's like being in the movie *Goonies* or *National Treasure*—there's usually a way out of the cave, even when you don't see it clearly at first sight. I'm not saying that everything in life offers a choice. I am saying that **most things do**.

"I'm not saying that everything in life offers a choice. I am saying that most things do."

My aim as a father is to teach my boys to seek out the truth and the better way—to know they have choices in life.

We all make poor choices. However, knowing we can control the choices that ultimately prove to be poor is far more hopeful than living a life decided by circumstance and fate. A brighter outlook suggests that we have the ability to make choices that will be right and good. We all like hearing the phrase, "Good choice!"

When you wake up tomorrow and consider what's for breakfast, ask, "Do I have a choice?"

HOOK #38

*Patience is
the pathway to growth.*

SOME WOULD SAY persistence is the pathway to growth—the stick-to-itiveness. I agree. Yet, persistence can hinder growth if you insist on pursuing something the wrong way.

For example, PayPal started as a company focused on cybersecurity (cryptography) and then moved into transferring money through PDAs. It wasn't until after much deliberation, trial and error, replacing leadership, and changing their service product (what they do) that they found their position in the marketplace. Of course, we now know PayPal as a household name for sending money online.

Here's another example: At twenty-two years old, golfer Sergio García was hailed as Europe's answer to Tiger Woods. At the time, he had the greatest potential of all the golfers in the world. During his climb to success, he decided to change his swing. Critics and peers all questioned his decision and vocalized their astonishment. Sergio explained that even though he was finding great success with his current approach, he noticed he lost a bit of control in high-pressure moments. His swing needed "too much rhythm," which required his body to be fully relaxed and unfazed. With higher aspirations in mind, he decided to make adjustments rather than continue on his current path. Sergio went on to win the Masters in 2017.

The listed definition of persistence is "firm or obstinate continuance in a course of action in spite of difficulty or opposition."

"When someone says, 'I don't want to start over,' they are more likely implying, 'I don't want to lose time.'"

Persistence is reasonable when you are confident that you are on the right track. **However, when results are not evident over time, it's wise to, at the very least, evaluate and question your course of action.** When someone says, "I don't want to start over," they are more than likely implying, "I don't want to lose time." **Often, we would rather be persistent towards a**

negative outcome just because we don't want to invest the time it would take to start over. We want results now!

When I was younger, I would get anxious rehearsing alone. My inability was frustrating, so I became impatient and began forcing my technique rather than trusting the process and focusing on my practice. I knew that to achieve my goals, I needed to be better. To get better, I needed to practice. When, and if, I could truly elevate my ability was an unknown. (I believed, but until it was evident, I wasn't sure.)

This uncertainty made my practice sessions stressful. I wanted to see immediate results. My need for immediacy hindered my progress. **The better alternative would have been to view the process as the result. The practice being the goal, rather than the result of the practice.** This perspective would have allowed the process to unfold at a natural pace rather than a forced and stressful one.

For example, let's take a look at singing. Singers practice to become better singers. That is the ultimate goal. Typically, singers who recognize they need to practice are aware of the difficult passages or lines in their songs. So, they practice those parts specifically. In this case, getting better at the identified phrase or line is the goal.

Singing comes naturally to many. However, most singers need to work on improving the elements that affect the sound of the note. These elements (just to name a few) are breath, posture, placement, shape of mouth, and ear training. Often, finding the best mouth shape or posture for breath support takes a bit of trial and error through practicing—patiently.

Again, the ultimate GOAL is to sing better. However, if at every turn you are checking the sound of the note when you should be experimenting with your breathing or mouth shape, you are practicing incorrectly and impatiently. The GOAL of the practice should be to breathe better, or stand more relaxed, or shape your mouth in an O rather than an E. Your intention should shift from the ultimate goal of "Does this sound good?" to the immediate goal of "What am I specifically practicing right now?" **If you know you are on the**

right path, then be patient and detailed with the practice. (By the way, process-oriented practice is quite common in athletics these days. Listen to sports radio covering your favorite team, and you will hear more than one reference on the topic.)

In truth, persistence and patience must work hand in hand to achieve any goal.

Simply stated, don't get so caught up in needing to see immediate results that you are unwilling to find the *best* way forward. First, be patient in determining if you are on the right path. Allow yourself the time to start over if needed. Second, once you are headed in the right direction, give yourself time to build a solid foundation.

Find your way and take your time. Be patient.

HOOK #39

Everything in nature
needs reinforcement, refueling,
and recharging. Even you.

LET'S PLAY A game. Think of anything, and I'll tell you (or I'll google it and then tell you) how it needs to be recharged, refueled, replaced, or given rest. Since I'm here and you are there, I will have to go for you.

Responses will be very simple and generalized. If you need more detail, feel free to look it up.

- **Bears:** It gets cold and they hibernate until it warms up.
- **Dolphins:** One half of their brain sleeps while the other keeps going.
- **Plants:** Can anticipate the rising of the sun and thrive in the light. At night they use this energy to grow.
- **Cell phones:** Will lose power in the middle of an important phone call unless charged.
- **Toddlers:** Will drive you nuts if they haven't had enough sleep.
- **Guitar strings:** Will snap if not changed regularly.
- **Drum heads:** Will tear if not changed regularly.
- **Light bulbs:** Burn bright, burn out, and need to be replaced.
- **Air filters:** Will take on too much dust and clog if not changed regularly.
- **Guitar amps and speakers:** Can get too hot and need air to function. No air and too hot, they shut down.
- **Vocal cords:** Too much use and they won't produce sound.
- **Cars:** Run out of gas.
- **Tennis shoes:** Gotta replace your kicks after a while. Soles wear thin and threads become tattered.
- **Dishes:** Need washing for reuse.
- **Grass:** Needs trimming.
- **Hair:** Needs trimming.
- **Fences:** Need mending over time.
- **Broken hearts:** Need time for mending.
- **Houses:** Need cleaning and new paint from wear and tear.
- **Clowns:** Need cleaning and new paint from wear and tear.

You get the point. Or maybe not—that list is a bit silly.

Our minds and bodies are just like anything else we share space with on this planet. If you believe the best way to go after your goals (professionally or personally) is by unrelenting doggedness without rest, you are mistaken. Somehow, we've been trained to accept ideas like "I'll sleep when I'm dead!" No thank you. I'll sleep tonight and then again for about an hour at two in the afternoon!

Philosopher Joseph Pieper said, "Leisure is only possible when we are at one with ourselves. We tend to overwork as a means of self-escape, as a way of trying to justify our existence." I can relate to that. Can you?

I've learned to accept the benefits of rest, relaxation, and rebirth. Again, the spaces between the notes are just as important as the notes themselves.

Take a break. Take a vacation. Take a nap.

The key word there is TAKE. When you take something, you are grabbing it—willfully.

Believe that taking your mind and body away from your most pressing concerns will be better for you in the long run.

Check out these quotes:

> "Hard work is the price we must pay for success." – Vince Lombardi
>
> "You do not pay the price of success; you enjoy the price of success."
> – Zig Ziglar

Notice that Lombardi didn't say "overwork" but simply "hard work." It's true, we all must work hard sometimes to achieve our goals. But what's the point of our riches if we are too beaten down and stressed to enjoy those riches every now and then?

So, I've amended Vince's quote: "Hard work, *with some rest,* is the price we must pay for success." – Vince Lombardi (and Matt Wilson)

HOOK #40

Find something frivolous and enjoyable that requires your complete attention and focus.

I PLAY VIDEO games. Specifically, I play Madden Football on my PlayStation. If I had the time, I would buy other video games and play more often. But I don't, so I don't.

I sometimes feel guilty about my gaming. I think, "You should be writing, reading, working out, cleaning the house, or doing something more productive." Yet, I know, for me, this is not always true.

I'm analytical. I'm competitive. I'm driven by a desire and a calling to do great things with my life. Although this drive is a blessing, at times it can be stressful and cause overthinking.

Back to my football video game. I can't stand to lose! (I need to work on how much I can't stand to lose when playing this game.) I play online, so I'm competing with people from all over the world. The online players are usually "boss level" (as my kids say), and playing competitively requires "skills." The game is challenging and requires my full attention. Attention I gladly give. (It's not like watching TV while scrolling Twitter.)

Some days the obligations of being a dad and business owner are so stressful that I think, "I need a distraction. Let's play some football!" It works. Playing my game is a welcome diversion.

Rarely does overthinking about something bring a solution. Ruminating typically causes anxiety and unproductive worry.

I recently read a great quote about this: "Worrying seems to be the responsible thing to do." (I don't recall where I saw this or who said it.)

"Stepping away from our daily concerns can bring about a fresh perspective."

Stepping away from our daily concerns can bring about a fresh perspective. You know, the "Go to bed and see how you feel in the morning" thing.

Also, rewarding yourself with something fun and frivolous creates balance in your life. (I only play the game at night when most of my responsibilities are taken care of.) Balance is good. Reward is good.

Find something you love to do that will demand your attention and give you respite from the daily grind. You will reduce stress, have a good time, and be more effective when you get back to work.

Yes, my advice here is to "Play video games!"

HOOK #41

*The big moments in life
are not always
the best moments.*

I WAS ON the football team in high school. I was a good athlete but too small to play high school football in Texas. If I'm being honest, I *believed* I was too small, which made me apprehensive. That, combined with the self-awareness a career (or even a scholarship) in football was not in the cards, made me a fringe player on the field. I liked the idea of being a football player (I love football). I didn't like the idea of risking my body. I stopped playing after tenth grade.

One moment I recall was at the end of my freshman year. The varsity and JV teams held spring practices that culminated with the Green and White game. It was a big deal, for sure. The day of the Green and White kicked off with a school-wide pep rally. Every player was to be introduced by the coach and paraded across the stage in their green or white jersey. With the last name Wilson, I sat and watched all of my teammates bathe in the glory as our young peers screamed familiar names and barked liked dogs for their buds. I remember sitting on the edge of my seat waiting to stand while coach Thomas grunted, "And at JV Quarterback, freshman Matt Wilson." Woof! Woof!

Yet, what coach actually said was, "And here is your BA Cougar football team!" He was done! He forgot about "JV quarterback, freshman Matt Wilson." Maybe now I would let things go, but back then, I stood up and quite sheepishly interrupted coach Thomas and said, "What about me?" Luckily, he remembered I was on the team, and we didn't have to have a discussion. (Or, even worse, an introduction.) He called my name, and I quickly made it across the stage…not quite how I imagined!

Big moments come with BIG expectations. These expectations are rarely based on reality and experience, but on what we *hope* for them to be. Big moments are like the opening tee shot at the company golf tournament. Everyone is watching, and you are not a golfer. There is a chance you will hit the ball just fine, but there's also a chance your attempt will be humbling (to put it nicely). Conversely, run-of-the-mill everyday moments in life are like you and your buds hitting the links on a Saturday afternoon—no big whoop but a lot of fun.

Little moments count just as much as big moments. Take them all in equally.

As an artist, I think I've lived most of my life waiting for the next big opportunity or accomplishment. Too many times, I stressed out over a "big gig" just to realize it was like any other. In the end, many proved to be kind of lame or disappointing in some fashion.

In one instance, the band was playing a huge gala, and we were going to sing my original song "Press On" with a children's choir to open the ceremonies. Not only was my song going to get some exposure, but we were supporting a good cause. Good vibes all around! Looking out at the one thousand or so people in attendance, I was ready to showcase my tune and kick some butt. (For a good cause, of course, and with kid backup singers.) The voice of God announced that the program was about to begin and for everyone to find their seat. Long story short, after about fifteen minutes of trying to get the mob to sit, we just had to start. Our big showcase was barely noticed. The children's choir had a tough time making it to the stage through the giant cocktail party. I bet some attendees wondered why there were even kids at the event. One guy handed a kid his empty drink and said, "Scotch and soda!" (Just kidding. That'd be funny, but didn't happen…I don't think.) I'm not sure anyone really knew we were even there. Quite fitting that we were singing a song called "Press On"! Am I right?!

It's just how it goes. Don't get me wrong, I've had so many big moments in my life go beyond my most hopeful visions. However, I'm too aware of how things can be quite disappointing if not tempered with reality. And reality confirms that if you give the perceived big moments in life more value than the average Tuesday, you're more likely to carry a nagging feeling of unhappiness.

Note that what is a big moment to me may not be to you. That goes for everyone. Movie stars are just as let down as the guy next door.

Yes, the coach forgot to introduce me at my first big football rally, and nobody stopped chatting to listen to my tune at the big gala. However, my boy just made a Christmas card telling me he is "getting braver" at playing piano in front of people and that he loves me.

Maybe that wasn't a *big* moment, but it was definitely a *best* moment.

HOOK #42

Expectations can be disruptive.

THINK BACK TO a time when you were looking forward to an event, gathering, or holiday. Now think about telling someone about that event. Can you recall saying, "I thought it would be different"?

I'm sure you can. We do this all the time. Our lives are filled with unmet expectations, and that's ok.

Yet, during a performance or presentation, unmet expectations can have consequences. When you create preconceived conditions in your mind for an event where you must perform, you rely on those conditions to meet your expectations for optimal success. That's ok if all goes according to your plan. However, it rarely does. So then what?

You thought the room would be bigger or the lighting more varied. Maybe there isn't a green room available or space for you to prepare and gather your thoughts. The meal you were promised is late or substandard. The audience is not as attentive as you had hoped. There's a negative vibe surrounding the setup and preparation of the space. I'm sure our grumblings could make an entertaining Twitter thread. There are certainly too many examples to list here.

> *"Disappointment is bound to affect your energy, focus, and execution.*
> *This can all be avoided if you simply balance your expectations."*

To be clear, this is not the same as, "I was told that it would be a certain way, and it's not." In the case of an unfulfilled promise, someone other than you is involved and can be held accountable for the distraction. In other words, it's somewhat out of your control, and your disappointment is justified. However, this is not an excuse for a poor performance. Read on.

In the case of imagined expectations, be wary.

Not only are you preparing for your show, speech, or event, you are also fighting the distraction of failed expectations. Disappointment is bound to affect your energy, focus, and execution. This can all be avoided if you simply balance your expectations. In fact, expect chaos.

I've learned that on bigger events and shows, the band will be late, the sound will have issues, the purchaser will act weird and distracted, the audience will not resemble what I first envisioned, and the list goes on. Really, my only expectation is that many things will be a distraction if allowed. I'm like Super Mario running, dodging, falling down holes, yet all the while pressing on (with a smile on my face).

Your objective is a good performance. Circumstances out of your control should not derail your purpose.

Eat the cold turkey wrap, grab the broken mic, and sing your heart out to the five folks sitting down and somewhat paying attention. Go get 'em!

HOOK #43

It's rarely as you imagined it would be.

MY THOUGHT HERE is not the same as my other groundbreaking, poignant, and life-changing take on unmet expectations. In that exploration, I was referring to how expectations can be a distraction to a performance (Hook #42).

I want to talk about the way we imagine everything to be.

Major life adventures like career, family, love, and friendship are deeply rooted in hope. We all carry a vision of how it's going to turn out. We aim for something, and that something is confined within a preconceived ideal of our own creation. More so, these goals are a product of how we were taught through stories, tradition, media, and just being an aware member of society. As Don Henley sang, "We've been poisoned by these fairy tales." A little dark, but you get it.

I'm certain a good chunk of our struggles come from dealing with disappointment. Think about it—we hurt because we thought we would achieve idealistic milestones that we simply created in our mind, and then fall short of those milestones just so. Or, we consider our reality a failure because it didn't follow the pattern laid out in our dreams.

When I became a father, I set new expectations for family gatherings and how my children would interact with my parents. I envisioned Norman Rockwell settings for holidays. We would all get together and laugh, love, eat, and share unforgettable picturesque moments. It never happened just like that. Someone was always in a bad mood, or the kids were too shy around Grammy and Pawpaw, or someone couldn't make it, or someone said something stupid that caused tension. Everything was just slightly off, and my inclination was to shout at the wind and excuse myself to grab an imaginary phone call!

I've learned to take it all in as it unfolds—all of it. I've also learned to enjoy the moments and blessings in life that have turned out the way I hoped for, or even those approximately so. I aim to be a good father and husband. I aim to be good at my job. I aim to be a good man in the eyes of God. I aim to have a life of order and purpose. I've learned to do my best to create an environment where my hopes can come to fruition. I've learned these things will not always be just so, and that's ok.

"Enjoy the freedom by letting go of how you imagined it all would be."

Be grateful for the people and moments you have to share the experience of life. Enjoy the freedom by letting go of how you imagined it all would be.

HOOK #44

People can change.
Never expect them to.

I'VE GIVEN A few examples of extremely talented but professionally challenged individuals I have worked with over the years. I can recall one who, no matter how many conversations we had about my concerns, continually repeated the problematic behavior—time after time.

There's an old saying that when someone shows you who they are, believe them. For example, if someone is always late, or a bit manipulative, lazy, or unreliable, these are probably true characteristics.

My struggle has always been believing in the hope and potential of people too much. I want to see someone change for the better, so I continue to believe that their expressed desires to do better are genuine.

Another common expression is, "Change is hard." Often, we use that phrase to describe circumstances *after* change has already taken place. Yet, the saying also refers to how difficult it is just to *begin* the process of change. **Making an effort to change a habit or point of view can be monumental. Most people don't have the drive or commitment.**

> ## "The saying 'Change is hard' also refers to how difficult it is just to begin the process of change."

I know two men that I work with now who confronted the need for change. One seems to have made great strides in turning his life in a positive direction. He's lost weight (in a good way), held on to a fantastic job, repaired his marriage, and invested his time in healthy hobbies that bring him joy. He's also admitted his mistakes from the past and showed gratitude and remorse to those affected most by his actions. I tried for years to encourage change with my words, lectures, threats, and pleading. Nothing worked until he decided to change.

My other friend may not follow the same path. He's currently in the state of "See, I'm doing better." This is typical for many after suffering some real-world consequences of their poor choices and behaviors. I hope he makes fundamental changes; however, I've witnessed this phase too often to be optimistic.

The best we can do is encourage those around us to make changes for the better. We also must understand that, although it is possible to rid one-self of disruptive habits and character flaws, it is quite difficult.

I'm still learning to relieve myself of the notion that I can provoke change in someone by motivation, encouragement, or by saying please. I've also learned I'm probably setting myself up for frustration and disappointment if I make plans and decisions based on how I hope someone will respond.

Be honest and realistic with your expectations of others. Be cautious if your plans and visions rely on someone to make significant changes. Even if that someone is you.

HOOK #45

You are not completely defined by what you do professionally. You are not what you do.

I STRUGGLE WITH this concept frequently. It's easy to see why. If my company created a widget, that widget would be me. My product is my voice, my face, my persona, my ideas, etc. It's challenging to separate my identity as a person from the success and failures of Matt Wilson the widget (performer).

Check this out though, when I choose to accept that I am not only a performer, but also a son, husband, father, and just a dude, I create an environment to be better at all of these simultaneously.

Think about it. If we are only what we do, then who are we if we fail at what we do? And what do we do with the other parts of our life?

Business is hard. Everyone will fail and miss the mark some of the time. Most will feel some sort of unfulfillment about dreams or goals left unmet (see Hook #43). If we allow ourselves to be defined and valued only by our career accomplishments, then we are indeed bound for misery.

My dad once joked, "What's better than money? More money!"

It's true though. Once we achieve a level of success, we need more. It's nearly impossible to shut off the ambition engine. The brief moment of joy and satisfaction dissipates and leaves us searching for our next accomplishment. The public is a "what have you done for me lately" sort. Bills are incessant. Life moves on no matter what, and the widget must be sold!

What do you think the one-hit wonder thinks about, their one hit or the fact they couldn't back it up with another? My guess is the latter.

If we are all consumed and solely identified by our work, then we are headed for burnout and discontent.

Also, earning an income to provide for one's needs is an inherent component of a career. That's a demanding responsibility, and for most, a life-long endeavor. Then add on to that an entire life's meaning! Good luck consistently performing under such expectations.

If I view every performance as not only a way to continue my career and support my family but also as a barometer of my value as a person, I am creating too much undue pressure on my immediate task. Every note becomes a representation of whether or not I have used my time on earth wisely, a measure of my value to society, and whether anyone will attend my funeral, and so on.... Dude, that's heavy!

So what if I have a bad show? I can still come home and be a good father and husband, just as I can center my emotions and give a good show after arguing with my wife. Being a good performer is important and defines me. Being a good husband is important and defines me. Being a good father is important and defines me. All equally! A balance of all makes it easier to be better at all. **Too much emphasis on one role and the others suffer from neglect, while the one in focus will eventually suffer from too much significance.**

For the ambitious, accepting this line of reasoning can be difficult. It becomes easier when you believe a balance in life will give you a greater chance of being the best at work.

Want to be better at selling more widgets? Go home and have dinner with your family!

HOOK #46

The pursuit of a meaningful life begins with seeking what is challenging.

WHEN MY WIFE and I decided to move for her new job, we both understood I would need to scale back my stage time. In addition to working more from home, I would take on added responsibilities with our two boys and manage the day-to-day around the house. The move also allowed me some freedom to do whatever.

I realized I'm nowhere near my "golfing days." I need challenges. I need to be useful. I have things I want to do and accomplish.

Yes, I find meaning in my role as a father and a husband. Though without the challenge of a professional pursuit, I am not balanced.

Having the road paved and traveled might sound welcoming. Yet, I believe one of our greatest desires is to be useful and have meaning. Accepting and taking on life's challenges is a surefire way to achieve both.

"One of our greatest desires is to be useful and have meaning."

A fundamental psychological theory that supports this idea is in Erik Erikson's stages of development. He lays out eight stages we all experience. Erikson theorizes that a person encounters a psychosocial crisis in each stage that can have a positive or negative outcome. A positive outcome at each stage sets us up for a healthy personality and a solid foundation for the next stage. My summary suggests stages one through six are self-centered—everything from learning how to walk and talk, finding a mate, finding a job, etc.

Then we get to stage seven, Generativity vs. Stagnation. Erickson defined Generativity as "a concern for and guiding the next generation." This is accomplished through teaching, parenting, mentoring, and by being productive at work. The opposite of this (Stagnation) leaves one with a feeling of dissatisfaction due to their inability or unwillingness to be productive and contribute.

The final stage is Integrity vs. Despair. Simply stated, we look back on life and see how we did. I find it interesting that the stage right before the final evaluation involves learning how to be meaningful to others. **One could infer that a well-rounded and properly developed person spends the first half of their life preparing to, ultimately, give hope and guidance to their fellow man.** If we don't successfully follow this development, then we are left with a sense of disappointment and regret.

So, the importance of finding meaning is science! It's a built-in test we all must take.

Accept the challenge to be challenged. It will serve you, and those around you, well.

HOOK #47

*If you truly believe
that a greater purpose
lies in your endeavor,
you will see that endeavor
to the end.*

AS A TEENAGER, I sensed I had a purpose in life. I was drawn to music, performing, and writing. While my peers were out on weekends blowing off steam, I would go to my father's church to play piano, sing, and write music. It was what I really wanted to do. I believed this was my calling. My belief kept me out of trouble and focused on the future. Although I had little training and was reinforcing bad habits and poor technique, I was still investing in my calling to be a performer.

At the time, I didn't know what I was doing, but I trusted I was part of a greater plan. I have maintained that direction throughout my life. Whether I am motivated by success, fear, competitiveness, money, or artistry, I am nonetheless motivated because of my calling.

While performing at Disney World, the shows would end at 2:00 a.m., so I followed a schedule of working at night and sleeping in the day. Right out of college, I was naive and uneducated about career opportunities in the music business, so I viewed my current profession as a passing one. Misguided, I lazily pursued law school. I would wake up around noon and force myself to study for the LSAT. I never thought deeply about being a lawyer; I just knew I needed a career, and friends told me I had a knack for thinking critically and communicating. All the while, without paying attention, I was starting to build a foundation for a life-long career in music and entertainment.

On the day of the LSAT, I traveled from Orlando to Tampa. I had performed the night before, so the 8:00 a.m. test time was inconvenient, to say the least. I walked out of the test after the first section. Disappointed, I called a friend back in Austin and told my tale of failure. I expressed my uncertainty about saving my chances for law school. Without knowing the weight and insight of his words, he said, "Maybe you don't want to be a lawyer."

Before that phone call, I believed you were either a superstar like Billy Joel or playing music as a hobby. Then, as if I'd found an unnoticed light switch in a poorly lit room, I realized I could pursue a career that matched my calling even if I wasn't going to be the next Billy, Elton, or Ray—and that I'd already started! It was around this time I earnestly began pursuing a career in music and entertainment.

Many spend years searching for direction. Throughout my life, I have been fortunate to follow a meaningful and profitable course. **For those still searching, I encourage you to make it your calling to find your calling.** I know! That sounds "super-motivational-speaker-y." Yet, propelled by pure and unfiltered motivation, a calling will change your life and bring you more meaning than money or other trappings "just a job" will offer. Why not aim for that?

I do not presume to tell you exactly how to find your calling. We all have our own path. However, I can say that I lose my car keys at least once a week, and I don't stop looking until I find them. Why? Because I know the keys are there, somewhere. Yes, I'm aware that finding car keys and finding a life's calling is a disproportionate comparison. **Focus not on the object, but the faith that the object is there to be found!**

Also, I believe we *just know* when we find people, matters, causes, and work that inspire passion. **So maybe, if we have faith that a calling is accessible, we will be more inclined to seek one out.**

I believe your calling is just waiting there to be found. Go look! More on this in the next Hook.

HOOK #48

Achieving Greatness:
Determine your most effective
and greatest skill.
Invest in opportunities
that allow you to showcase
that ability. Repeat.

WHAT ARE YOU good at? I mean, really good at! Take time to answer this before you move on.

There are a handful of skills I use in my profession. The two most obvious are playing the piano and singing. Over the course of my career, I have become quite capable at both. I'm also a songwriter and a producer of shows and songs. I have a knack for management, and I am interested in the business affairs of my industry.

Still, my greatest talent is my ability to engage an audience. This ability has been a gift my entire life. I'm not here to compare to anyone else, nor am I singing my own praises. I am merely pointing out something I had to realize to find peace and a proper aim for my endeavors.

For many years, I struggled with inconsistency. I would have fantastic performances, but I couldn't find a way to reproduce that energy in a controlled production (video shoot, audio recording, musical, etc.).

This struggle was most evident during my time in *Movin' Out*. How could a great performer not thrive in such an environment? The disparity began to eat away at my confidence and provoke anxiety. As time moved on, I would compare myself to my peers and wonder why they were finding success and I wasn't. (I was happy for them and concerned for myself.)

My concern stemmed from the belief that I had something special to offer, and I was disappointed that I was not meeting my potential.

I grappled with this matter for many years and suffered the consequences.

Then one day I realized I was promoting and leading my strategies with the wrong skills. Sure, I was a good piano player, but not the best, and playing wasn't the best I had to offer. Sure, I was a good singer, but not the best, and singing wasn't the best I had to offer. Although these two skills were the foundation of my profession, my true gift was my ability to entertain, engage, communicate, and inspire.

As long as I chose a path where I only featured my ability to play and sing, I would probably fall short of my aim for greatness. Why? Because, compared to the absolute very best professional singers and piano players in the world, I'm just average. This hurts to say, but it's true.

So, I changed my business strategy. My revised "mission statement" is to seek out opportunities where I can showcase my ability to entertain, engage, communicate, and inspire while utilizing my ability to play, sing, and write.

What are the effects of this approach? There are three:

1. I've created a more sustainable business model. Peddling something great is more effective than peddling something that is just ok.

2. I've set my goals on a more realistic path. If greatness is my aim, then I'd better have something I believe to be extraordinary to offer.

3. I'm at peace. I've accepted my limitations and strive to make them better. Yet, I aspire to no longer unfairly compare myself to others who have similar talents but different strengths. Nor do I measure myself against an idea of what I thought I was supposed to be. Sure, I may be recognized along the way for some of these above-average skills and God-given talents. However, relying on and featuring those abilities is a strategy destined for disappointment and insecurity. My aim is greatness, so I must showcase my *great* talents. Why drive slow in the middle lane when I know I can be a race car? I see where the turbo button is on this machine and I'm gonna use it! Over and over and over.

Don't neglect any of the skills required to do whatever it is you do. However, take the time to discover your number one skill and spotlight when possible.

It's going to be great!

Here are a few steps to help you get started with the "What am I really good at?" process:

1. **Consider all.** Let's imagine, using a real-life example, that what you do involves conceptualizing new ideas, organizing budgets, and implementing plans. Those plans typically include sales calls, social media campaigns, and convention presentations. In this exercise, you should consider all of these tasks and responsibilities.

2. **Eliminate most**. Continuing from step one, you believe you are *best* at coming up with ideas and formulating strategy behind the scenes, so you gravitate to that. Plus, you enjoy the leadership role. However, what you are *good* at is the sales part. Just *good*, but not *best*. And sales is not the best you have to offer. So, eliminate sales from contention and focus on opportunities to formulate ideas and strategy.

   - Note, eliminating is the hard part. Admitting you are just ok at something can be difficult.

   - Also note, this step should be honest and pragmatic, not wishful. This is not an exercise on what you *hope* to be really good at!

3. **Listen and observe**. Your audience, customers, managers, and peers will respond, react, and often tell you when you are really good at something. Pay close attention to what that "something" is—it's working! Also, compare successes and disappointments. Were you able to present your *best* or just *good*?

4. **Showcase**. Now that you have identified what you think you're really good at, focus your efforts on opportunities showcasing that skill. If you choose correctly, your work will be inspired, and results will follow.

COURAGE & FEAR

Managing your anxieties

HOOK #49

Look out!
Anxiety is contagious.

ONE OF MY most trusted counselors once said, "Anxiety is like crabgrass. It will spread."

My family came to see me during my first week on Broadway. The lights were bright for all of us. I was very much finding my footing in the new world, and things were not perfect. After my second or third show, I met with the musical director to review my performance. He needed improvements and wanted them immediately. (Broadway is a harsh and bottom-line world!)

No one in my family was familiar with Broadway protocol, so we were left with taking the criticism and learning to adapt at the same time. My caring father said, "Well, are they going to fire you?"

He didn't mean to overreact. He was anxious about his son's career, and his irrational thoughts were leading him to the worst possible outcome. I would be lying if I were to tell you that I was level-headed and rational. His anxiety quickly opened the door to all sorts of thoughts that maybe-could-possibly happen. My anxiety latched on to his, and we created an anxiety bonfire!

I wasn't fired by the way.

Be diligent in what you allow your mind to see and hear.

Only listen to those you trust when it comes to matters that are important and can affect your performance and execution. Instruct them to be honest and realistic. **Learn to identify communication based on anxiety and what-ifs.**

When you sense you are in a conversation or situation loaded with anxiety, remove yourself.

Mark Twain (we think) said, "I am an old man and have known a great many troubles, but most of them never happened."

Why allow yourself to be affected by anxiety for no reason? Focus on your task and technique. Encourage your advisors and partners to do the same.

HOOK #50

Play one song at a time.

ONE COMMON SIGN of anxiety is foreshadowing: the tendency to brace one-self and mull over impending danger or a pitfall.

I'm reminded of those times onstage when I'm cruising along and playing a tune just fine. At the same time, I'm fretting over a more difficult section of the song drawing near. More often than not, my anticipation turns to foreshadowing. The doomed section is now even more difficult, and I'm also distracted from the passage of the song currently underway. Some level of failure at this point is unavoidable.

Foreshadowing is a perfect word in this instance. Authors typically use foreshadowing to build up tension and offer a hint of something bad that will happen in the future. The foreshadowing doesn't show how it will happen, just that it WILL happen.

Being mindful of a more difficult passage ahead is anticipation. You can stay in the moment and allow the thought of what's to come to pass through, without concern. Again, that's anticipation. However, fretting over what you've determined to be inevitable sets you up for failure—most of the time. That's foreshadowing.

Stay in the moment. Connect with the words you are speaking or singing. Feel the spaces in between the notes. Give "now" the same amount of respect and focus you know "later" will require.

A "trap game" is when a team believes their upcoming opponent is not as formidable as others they will face down the road; consequently, their preparation is not as thorough. Rather than just following the standard practice routine with enthusiasm and attention to detail, the team or individual's overconfidence leads to half-hearted preparation. Often, this results in a loss to the perceived weaker opponent. Thus, they were "trapped" into believing they were a better team.

You get it. Sing this song now and that song later. Play these notes now and those notes later. Play this team now and that team later.

Play one song at a time.

HOOK #51

Regard negative thoughts
as trees passing on a highway.
They are in view and
seem to be moving toward you.
Soon, they will pass and be gone.
All the while, you are the one
driving the car.

THOUGHTS ARE POWERFUL. Without a full deep dive, try to recall a time in your life when you felt Worry, Uncertainty, Doubt, Dread, Shame, or Anxiety. Was this feeling caused by a real, tangible event affecting your life? Or was it just "all in your head," as they say?

A working musician cannot always rely on the promise of opportunity and guaranteed work. I, too, have experienced the uncertainty, worry, and anxiety of staring at a blank calendar. (Knowing me, I probably started to question my ability too!) As I sit here now, I can say everything worked out fine. My thoughts were a healthy reaction to my situation. Not having work is a legitimate concern and fear. One needs a good portion of that concern to motivate and propel forward.

What about when we have random, negative thoughts sparked by our imagination, a wandering mind, a strange dream, or an awkward conversation?

When I'm giving too much meaning to my random thoughts, my internal monologue goes something like, "Why did I think that? Does this have some deep underlying meaning? Why do I keep thinking about messing up? Is something really wrong here?" At this point, my thoughts will inevitably materialize into a perceivable reaction. For example, I'll carry a sense of depression that affects my day and relationships, or I will make a mistake in my performance.

"Over time I've learned that a thought can be just that—a thought."

Over time I've learned that a thought can be just that—a thought. It doesn't have to be anything more than something passing through my mind.

I've learned to stop judging and evaluating everything on my "mind's TV." Eventually, the thought and the residue trailing behind fade into a vague memory. Most importantly, I've learned how to minimize the impact of unwanted thoughts. I let them pass.

THE PASSING TREE

You are driving, and you see the trees on the side of the road. They appear to be approaching. You are now in line with them, and they are in line with you. Quickly, now you pass them by. If you choose to look back, they are still in your rearview mirror. At some point, you are so far down the road that you cannot see them any longer. The only way to experience the trees again is to turn around and drive by once more.

I guarantee that for unwanted random thoughts, applying this analogy works! Sure, we all have meaningful passing thoughts worth examining. **However, for the analytical types and control freaks out there, let some stuff go!** Life is hard enough and filled with genuine problems. **When in your control, aim for Peace of Mind, Certainty, Self-Confidence, Hope, Forgiveness, and Mindfulness.** (We are all in control more than we realize—we have a choice! Hook #37)

How many branches were on the last tree you passed on the highway? That's my point! You don't know and don't care. Drive on by, my friend.

HOOK #52

A wrestled thought grows stronger.

IMAGINE YOU HAVE stumbled into an argument with your significant other. The deeper the discussion, the higher the tension, and the greater chance of something regretful being said. The argument loses focus as past resentments and irritants find their way to the surface. This scenario is an example of when we could use the phrase "everything but the kitchen sink!"

On the other hand, if you resist the urge to win the argument and walk away, you might resolve the issue quickly and peacefully without all the bickering. (Like, it really isn't a big deal that the forks are prong-up in the dishwasher, and it's not a big deal to place them in prongs down! OKAY? Okay!)

In performance situations (and in my daily life), I face random and unwanted thoughts all the time. If I choose to actively resist them, then I am focusing my attention on the negative distraction. I am now having an argument with the thought. *You are gonna mess up!* "No I'm not!" *That part is coming up, and you are gonna fail!* "No, I don't think so…Why, do you think so?" You get the point.

Desperately fighting negative thoughts will give them strength. Calmly ignore unwanted thoughts. Think about the good stuff!

In general, it seems to bear out that by focusing on the things that bring us joy, comfort, love, and enthusiasm, we set ourselves up for a better chance at success. For example, studies show that employees who have meaningful personal lives perform better at work, and counselors encourage patients suffering from addiction to find someone or something to live for other than themselves.

More specifically, during a performance or presentation, I choose to not fight the negative thoughts. Rather, I choose to think of something that gives me joy (my sons, for example). My devotion to Carter and Harry lifts me out of bed each day with determination. That love can also be a comforting diversion when the stage lights are bright, and my mind is wandering into doubt.

Choosing not to resist the unwanted thoughts and purposely injecting a positive thought will make the worry fade away.

HOOK #53

*Courage is not
the absence of fear,
it's the willingness
to face it.*

AS I SIT staring at my computer screen, waiting for the following words to come together just right, the term "real talk" lingers in my mind. *Real talk* is a succinct way to say, "I'm about to be candid." So…

Real talk: Millions of people struggle daily with anxiety in their personal and professional lives. Although mostly hidden, anxiety is as real as a broken bone—can't see it, but you can feel it. The resulting fear and physical manifestations are often irrational and inexplicable. You can't just "be tough and get over it." You need knowledge and tools to manage the effects. If anxiety had a club, I would be a dues-paying, card-carrying member. Early in my adult life, I became aware of my "membership." At that moment, I accepted that my anxiety was a reason for a handful of individual failures and not an excuse. This realization gave me hope. I chose to learn how to regulate and transcend my anxiety rather than suffer as a victim. This challenge is a lifelong battle I've committed to taking head-on, and each day I carry the faith that I will overcome.

I don't take responsibility for having anxiety; I do take responsibility for how I respond.

My jump from barroom to Broadway was tough. Given the opportunity of a lifetime, I was discouraged by my persistent struggle. I couldn't understand why I wasn't *brave* enough just to let go of the fear.

At the time, I met twice a week with a counselor to discuss how my anxiety made me worry about messing up, failing my bandmates and the cast, correction from the suits in New York, and losing my job. I wasn't afraid of performing. I was afraid of failure and feeling the effects of the anxiety during my performance—the shortness of breath, sweaty palms, and cluttered mind. I was putting way too much pressure on my performances (reference Hook #16), but I had yet to understand that I had a choice in the matter.

One day, my counselor said, "Matt, you are one of the bravest people I know." I was taken aback and asked him to explain. He said, "Every night you get onstage and do your job in the face of legitimate and irrational fears.

At times, your discomfort level can be unbearable, but you push through. That's not being afraid. That's being courageous!"

A variety of stats show a World War II fighter pilot's life expectancy could be anywhere from seventeen seconds to a 60% chance of survival. A myriad of factors played a role in whether a pilot faced sure death or had a glimmer of hope. Whatever the case, when the pilot climbed aboard to take to the sky, he knew for sure the odds were against his return. I can say with near certainty that most of the pilots were afraid. Yet they soared against the fierce blowing wind of fear and courageously fulfilled their duty.

Now, singing some tunes at a bar or on Broadway, or giving a presentation at work, does not come close to facing death in a war. However, fear is fear. Hurt is hurt. Disappointment and shame can be devastating, no matter the dose.

For those struggling with anxiety and fear, know that when you simply show up, when you perform the task at hand despite your fear, you may seem to be insecure and afraid. Yet, in truth, you are proving to be quite determined and courageous.

Maybe accepting this will allow the fear to subside in time. Your extreme and painful willingness to be courageous, over and over again, will eventually pay off, and these things that cause such great fear and anxiety will taper.

Believe that, courageously!

BUSINESS

*Taking care of business and
fine-tuning how we work*

HOOK #54

*Humor is often
a distraction during
a business conversation.
Be cordial and calm,
not funny.*

MY GOOD FRIEND Joe once told me he hated jokes. I asked him why, and he said it's because they are rarely funny, often offensive, and require, in most cases, that you pretend to laugh. (He was annoyed by that small social burden.)

Growing up as a preacher's son, I recall an old memory. A group of ministers gathered together for a serious theological discussion, and one posed the question, "What stretches further, skin or plastic?" Interrupted, yet inquisitive, the gathering waited for an answer. "Skin," said the jokester; "'Cause the Bible says Joseph tied his ass to a tree and walked a mile." After an uncomfortable chuckle or two and then a refocusing, the old gag proved to serve every purpose other than what was intended.

Humor often relies on sarcasm, irreverence, and vulgarity. At the very least, there is always the possibility that you will derail the conversation from the topic at hand or, at worst, offend. One hundred percent of business calls start with a weather report and an undesired stand-up routine. Who has time for all this? Hyperbole, I know. Yet, a cooperative and pleasant disposition is all that is necessary to conduct your business.

Be at ease and focused when doing business. Not funny.

HOOK #55

*Unless unavoidable,
"Don't fire.
Just don't rehire."*

– Mike Mordecai

MY MANAGER OF many years taught me this lesson. Contract labor and for hire labor dominate all forms of business. Relationships are vital. When things are not working out, it's best to just move on without the ceremony that accompanies "You are fired" or the damage caused by taking away work.

"Protect your business relationships, even the ones that seem to have lost their value."

When feasible, stop contracting the individual for additional work without explanation and damage. This preserves the relationship for the future.

Circumstances change, and people can be mutually valuable to unforeseen future endeavors. **Protect your business relationships, even the ones that seem to have lost their value.**

HOOK #56

The relationship is often bigger than the project.

IT'S COMMON TO feel so wrapped up in a project that the completion becomes the singular goal at all costs. Every nuance, expenditure, and detail are of the utmost importance. This weight of responsibility can cause tension among bandmates and team members. Disagreements can arise and cause irreparable damage if left unmanaged.

As time passes, a new and even more important project is at hand. All the while, the old project doesn't seem as life-altering. The overbudget expense or the color of the font is now trivial when looking back.

"There are many projects, but there is only one team."

Enthusiasm is vital to creative synergy yet can lead to healthy disagreements. Manage the drive and enthusiasm so they don't overwhelm the relationships.

There are many projects, but there is only one team.

HOOK #57

Never let money
stand in the way
of a valued relationship.

ONE OF MY biggest blunders as a business owner involved a cancellation by one of my band members. This band member was a vital piece to a particular show, and she had to cancel. In the moment, my business logic suggested I should make her take financial responsibility for finding a viable sub. My position did not align with hers, and we found ourselves at a crossroads.

I immediately resigned my take on the matter and apologized.

Rather than attempt to assert my case, I agreed that I chose the wrong path and admitted to my error. I was not going to let a financial matter interfere with a valuable working relationship and friendship.

> ## "I was not going to let a financial matter interfere with a valuable working relationship."

The disagreement exposed other matters that needed the opportunity for discussion, and we were able to reestablish her agreement with the band for the betterment of everyone involved.

If money were my bottom line here, she would no longer be in the band and probably no longer a friend.

That would be a shame!

I aim to apply these principles when it comes to money and my valued relationships:

- Pay contract labor on time and fairly.
- Be flexible and patient collecting money owed. Unless you have legitimate reasons to believe otherwise, you will get paid. Be calm. Use aggressive collection as a last resort.
- If you suspect a genuine need, be willing to forgive debts between friends.

- Offer to pay friends for their professional services. Do not assume they will offer you a deal. Be grateful if they do!

- Learn the difference between investing in someone (work without pay/smaller fees) and offering services strictly for hire (full rate). More importantly, learn when to offer one or the other. I tend to *invest* in the relationships that I see have long-term promise. In these cases, I am lenient with my fees.

- Accommodate business partners and clients who are struggling financially. When feasible, be willing to temporarily adjust fees to help weather their storm.

- Most times, the better choice is to protect the relationship over winning the financial disagreement. Promote compromise.

HOOK #58

Never order food on break.
You won't have time
to eat it.

RELATIONSHIPS ARE ALL about routines. Our lives are like a play. We all have roles that fit within a developed and ingrained script we unconsciously follow as we act out life with those nearest. If you enjoy a relationship, stay on script. If you want to change something about a relationship, change your role. Respond in a way that affects the normal routine. You change your line; they must follow suit.

Over time, I noticed the smallest of routines with my wife. Without fail, it seemed every time I was preparing to leave for work, she would ask me to handle a small chore or two. "Hey, on the way out, can you take out the trash?" or "Before you leave, can you tighten that loose screw on the door handle?" or "Can you go find the boy's shoes, so they are ready when we need them?" The chore was always perceived to be quick and could be anything at all.

One of my character traits is accommodating, so I would oblige. Then, also without fail, the chore would become an ordeal. I couldn't find both shoes, or the trash bag would leak, or the screw on the doorknob needed a smaller screwdriver than the one I could readily find. *Who's been using my tools?!*

Rather than focusing on the task at hand (preparing to depart and perform a show), I was now distracted and committed to a trivial task. (Trivial in the moment. I mean, the boys need their shoes, but I don't need to be on "shoe duty" as I'm heading out the door.)

Ultimately, I found a polite way to say, "Not now, but I will later." In doing so, I

- prioritized what was most important at the time,
- acknowledged that whatever was being asked of me would be a priority later,
- potentially steered away from unnecessary frustration, and
- removed a staple item off of the Reoccurring Argument List. (This list can get pretty long at times! Can I hear it from the married folks?)

Let's talk about my band for a minute (segue). The real, primary function of a band leader is food manager (wink).

Food is essential on a gig. It really is. The band and production team need to eat. That being said, the meal is not the priority. (Sarcastically, I muse on the idea that musicians act as if they studied for years perfecting their craft, only to get hired to go eat. Did I mention that food is important to the band?!)

It's my job to make sure the band eats *before* the gig. Coordinating meals on a break never (maybe-sometimes-but-really-rarely-so-never) works. You can count on the food arriving late, and then the band has only a few precious moments to cram down their meals. There is no way you can ask the band to get back onstage before they finish eating. (Did I mention that food is important to the band?) The talent buyer, manager, or client is now wondering why the band is not back onstage. "We are eating, of course." What a pain in the gut for all involved.

If food is provided on a gig, talk about what you are eating and when with the client during negotiations. Unless there is a long break during the performance, insist on having the performers' meal before the show. Trying to coordinate all of this on the day of the gig is complicated and distracting.

Also, consistently lobbing inquiries about food to the client at the gig will give the impression that your priorities are out of line. Eat and have a good show—in that order.

"Adding even the simplest of tasks to a focused and laid-out plan can be impactful."

I believe you can see that I am suggesting we all stay focused on the task at hand. What is important right now? What should take priority now? Are we going to work, or are we fixing the doorknob? Are we playing a gig, or are we having a dinner meeting?

Adding even the simplest of tasks to a focused and laid-out plan can be impactful.

If the doorknob needs repair, then prioritize it and put it in the script. Make it part of the plan. Just as feeding the band is essential and arranged beforehand.

Next time you feel the last-minute urge to pick up the dry cleaning on the way to the meeting (because it's on the way), say to yourself, "Don't order food on break!"

It's not in the script.

HOOK #59

Don't count tips in public.

I TRY TO follow this rule; however, sometimes it's impractical.

If you deal in an industry where tips are shared, make an effort to count away from your public's eye. Sorting through your loot in private is well mannered.

Let's dive deeper for a moment. I do my best to give my audience the impression that my single goal is to entertain and elicit emotion. I diligently remind myself that my motives must remain pure to achieve the best performance. If I'm merely there for the money, then my show will suffer (Hook #72).

I've always believed that focusing any aspect of my stage persona on money makes the show about money. If I want to move my audience to tears of joy and sadness, laughter and love, well, we know what The Beatles sang—"Can't Buy Me Love."

When I first moved to New Orleans, I encountered many challenges one faces moving to a new city. One of these was finding trusted repairmen for appliances and such. My AC was struggling to cool during the first "Dude… it's sooo hot here!" month of August. Keep in mind, I'm from Texas and can stand the heat. However, I was accustomed to super-charged AC winds like in the Lone Star State. My NOLA unit wasn't cooling my Longhorn hide. So, I called around looking for help. My initial search attracted folks that wanted to sell me a new unit rather than fix the perfectly-good-all-but-this-one-thing unit I had. They didn't want to help me with my problem. They only wanted to make money off my current vulnerability. Good for them, but they didn't get my business!

I eventually found someone who identified my issue and fixed it. I am now a loyal customer.

Whatever service you offer, aim to focus on the service, not the compensation. Draw attention to your talent and product, and the money will follow. Then count your money in private.

HOOK #60

Compliment your peers.

EVERYONE LIKES TO hear compliments. People who give presentations or perform are especially fond of them. Again, performing in any capacity is personal (Hook #34). Telling someone they did a good job or you enjoyed their performance is nice and encouraging. If you need more motivation to do so, a genuine compliment will endear you to your fellow artists or coworkers.

I know the music business (all business, for that matter) is quite competitive, and it's easy to feel moments of jealousy or a twisted pleasure in being critical of others' work. However, envy and faultfinding are counterproductive to one's success and a hindrance to creativity. Find joy in your peers' success, and they just might find joy in yours. In any case, you will feel good about helping someone along their journey.

I want as many professional opportunities as possible. However, I can only be in one place at a time, and even I grow tired of my schtick. Variety is good for a community.

Support your fellow artists and peers. Celebrate their success and achievements.

Focus on making your own way. You will find it all works together in the end.

HOOK #61

Form a trusted team and use them for counsel.

WHEN NEGOTIATING, I'LL have moments when I question my proposal, vacillate on what I should offer, wonder if I said something right or wrong, and fight the urge to not overthink the whole deal. I would be a terrible negotiator if I shared these thoughts with the other side.

In truth, I do share these thoughts. I just share them with my team and *not* the client. I also go round and round about photos for the band, mixes for new tunes, songs to add to the set, and should I wear a hat or not. It goes on and on! Often, just having someone to talk to is the key that unlocks a decision. I've maintained the same trusted advisors for almost twenty years now. Along the way, I've added some and married one.

Build a team and use them.

I can recall one instance where we invited two potential clients out to a show hoping they would book the band for future engagements. A week or so went by after the show without any word. I was disappointed, trying to figure out what we were doing wrong, and grumbling to my team. All the while, I kept communication with the clients to a minimum. I wasn't going to let them know I was concerned at all. In the end, both clients chose the band for their events. By using my team as a sounding board for my concern, I avoided appearing to be desperate.

Most successful businesses have a solid team for counsel and operation. Do your best to build one.

HOOK #62

*If you are willing
to hire a producer,
let 'em produce.*

I STARTED RECORDING original songs in 1992. I consistently utilized the services of a producer up until 2015. Most of my recent recording projects have been self-produced or co-produced with the aid of my band.

In 2014, I recorded and released a four song EP produced by the renowned Scott Mathews. During the recording process, I noticed I was offering too much input by wanting to explore every little idea in my head. I wasn't allowing him to do his job effectively with the continued suggestions. So, I decided to be highly selective with my comments related to the production.

Sure, all ideas are worth exploring. However, at some point, you could be overriding the person you hired to *have the ideas*. I hired Scott because I trusted his vision. Therefore, I was going to let him do his job. In the end, the record sounded great, and the reviews were positive.

Moving forward, if I have a pre-determined direction on future projects, I need to

1. **State my intention of co-producing at the onset of the project. (This was the path chosen on my last record.)**

2. **OR, don't hire a producer and do it myself. (I chose this path on a handful of recent singles.)**

When I see the need to have a different perspective on my work, I will hire a producer.

And I will let them produce!

HOOK #63

*Mind your own business.
When someone is unable
or unwilling to perform,
the show must go on.*

EARLY IN MY career, I became close friends with one of the owners of the club where I performed. Just being around him gave me access to the inner workings and issues that club owners encounter.

He would often say, "No one can hold me over a barrel!"

In the event an employee quit, called in sick, or didn't show, he believed he could cover any and all services and responsibilities, if needed. He aimed to know it all—cash registers, bartending, equipment repair, floor management, etc. If in a bind, he could do it, and the business wouldn't suffer during the transition. Or, at the very least, he would know enough about the operation or task to direct the right person to handle the job.

Throughout my career, I've had managers write contracts and manage the books. I've relied on engineers to edit videos and mix audio. I've asked agents to negotiate and book performances. I've counted on production teams to deliver, set up equipment, and run sound and lights for performances. These are just a sample of my operating needs, and I can do them all. In fact, many of them I do now, as I have moved my management team away from daily operations.

As I cover in Hook #68, a healthy business has targeted delegation. However, when resources (time, talent, money) are limited, there's still work to be done. Learn how to manage and operate as much of your business as possible.

I cannot think of many tasks I cannot do related to my business and performances. I'm a grade A jack-of-all-trades in Matt Wilson Entertainment. No need to find the barrel, y'all.

What about you? Are you barrel proof?

HOOK #64

*More often than not,
you have time to
make a decision.
Use it.*

OVER TIME, I have learned that the space between notes is just as important as the notes themselves. Excitement and emotion can cause a player to rush through the space within a tune. Consequently, the song is hurried and loses its groove.

We can use this as an analogy for making decisions.

I'm sure you can relate to a time when you made a hasty decision and changed your mind after the fact. Often, important decisions are not required immediately. Yet, sometimes we make decisions before they are necessary. Then we find ourselves in uncomfortable situations or reflections of regret.

I once hastily committed to a new band member after our longtime drummer retired. One really good show convinced me that we had found our new guy. After a few weeks and numerous confrontations, I realized I'd made a mistake. I couldn't get rid of the guy fast enough, yet I wanted to protect the relationship. If I had waited to offer a commitment, the exit would have been easier, quicker, and less stressful. (Heard of a "trial period," Matt?) In truth, I had plenty of time to decide on our future drummer. I just didn't use it.

Experience brings clarity. Experience builds through time. When you can, use time to your advantage in making clear decisions.

HOOK #65

*Discuss your goals
and ideas with counsel.
Do not promote your
ideas to the public.
Announce accomplishments.*

I ONCE WORKED with a guy who made sure everyone was aware of his potential "deals in the works." He believed by promoting what might happen, he would garner the same attention as if it did happen. These deals rarely came though, if ever. This was his form of self-promotion.

I get it! We need to promote ourselves to be successful. It's almost required in these days of social media. If it doesn't make Facebook or Instagram, did it really happen? When success seems elusive, just announcing that you might have something to celebrate gives you a small sense of achievement—even though nothing has been accomplished.

I also understand the need to share goals. One way publicly traded companies elicit and excite shareholders is to announce plans. These *plans* are actually *accomplishments* (even though the final product has not been manufactured). In this case, the company has decided on a direction and allocated resources toward this vision. For example, when Ford Motor Company announced the decision to manufacture an electric F-150, they also set the availability date two years down the road. The decision to build the truck *was the accomplishment*. Shareholders needed to know the company's direction. If Ford were not confident they could manufacture an electric F-150, their plan would simply be an *idea*. Plans that are just ideas should not be publicly disclosed to influence the marketplace. A company that continually promotes unrealized ideas will lose the public's trust and attention. **Bottom line, discern between plans that are *accomplishments* and plans that are *ideas*.**

What eventually happened with the guy above is that we stopped listening. We started to realize he was "all hat and no cattle," as they say.

> ## "One of the many unstated commitments a team offers is the willingness to listen to hopes and dreams."

As you know, I believe in forming a trusted team (Hook #61). One of the many unstated commitments a team offers is the willingness to listen to hopes and dreams. A team should also be privy to potential deals and negotiations. I believe it's imperative to be able to talk about matters just to get it all out—kind of like the detective who scatters the crime scene pictures all over the floor so he can get a bird's-eye view.

However, Columbo wouldn't go to the local IHOP and spread the pics out on the table for all to see.

Celebrate your achievements with your public, coworkers, and peers. Save your ideas and negotiations for your team.

You don't want your audience to stop listening.

HOOK #66

When you ask for someone's opinion, be prepared to hear it.

ESTABLISHING A TEAM you can confide in and draw counsel from is imperative to any successful venture. When seeking out opinions, consider the following:

- **Who do you trust?** Unreliable opinions can be off target, uninformed, uninspired, and offered without your best interests in mind.

- **What is your motive?** Are you genuinely wanting an outside opinion, or are you merely looking for someone to reinforce what you believe?

- **Are you prepared to be influenced?** Opinions received will have an effect in some manner, great or small. Be prepared to discern the critique.

For years, I sought counsel from someone I trusted personally but not entirely professionally. I began to notice I would leave business conversations frustrated and in complete disagreement. I determined that hearing their opinion on certain issues was more detrimental and distracting than helpful. It put me in a sour mood and made me question things that didn't need changing. It wasn't that I rejected differing opinions. It was, ultimately, that I didn't trust their experience enough to consider the advice.

Don't ask your uncle Bob what he thinks of your album artwork or Jim in engineering if the sales brochure is tight unless you want to be influenced by their opinion.

HOOK #67

*If you take the wedding gig,
give it your all!*

I'M NOT EXACTLY sure when the act of performing at a wedding gained such an unwarranted stigma among musicians as being unworthy of our divine talents. Musicians are a funny lot. We live within a code that, sometimes, is a detriment to our livelihood.

THE MUSICIAN'S RESPECT LADDER

Top Rungs

The most respected among the group are the ones who play their originals. (That's our term for original songs—songs written by the performer.) That respect is warranted for those who have figured out a way to make a living off original material.

Middle Rungs

Next on the respect ladder are the jazz cover guys. ("Cover" is our term for a song that is not original to the artist performing—the performer didn't write it.) These guys didn't write the tunes, but because the songs are more challenging to play, the performers get more street cred (credibility).

Bottom Rungs

On the respect ladder's lower rungs are the rock/pop/country/R&B cover bands. There's even a hierarchy in this group, but I'll spare you. At any rate, these cats ("cats" is our term for musicians) play famous cover songs everyone has grown to love and adore. These cats make the most local bread ("bread" is our term for money).

So, to be clear in this instance, the majority of musicians making enough money to maintain a career and pay their bills with their skills are mostly playing shows their peers find compromising to the integrity of the craft— only for money. Or, "that cat is just taking the hit for the bread, dude." ("Hit" is a term for gig...ok, I'll stop!)

At one point, many famous musicians wouldn't allow their music to be played on commercials. That still may be a thing. However, in this new business climate, having your song accompany a cheeseburger on radio or TV makes one an accomplished songwriter. Times do change.

At any rate, this complicated web of *who is doing what with their craft and how* can infiltrate the mind of the performer. If the CAT is more concerned with maintaining his CRED on the street, then that CAT probably won't respect the gig that's paying the BIG BREAD. That lack of respect will affect the performance. (At this point, I go back to "if you don't want to play the gig you were hired to play, don't take the gig." Hook #9)

So, back to the wedding.

For some reason, again, the wedding band "gets no respect"—as Rodney Dangerfield would have said. It's like a double shot of compromising. Not only is the band playing cover tunes, but at a wedding! Lame, dude!

This line of thought is just wrong. First of all, it takes a lot of practice and polish to be a good, competitive wedding band. The musicianship needs to be spot on, and the performers need to know how to entertain. Second, the pay is typically more per musician than your average club date. Making money with your craft is a good thing, guys! And to that point, most importantly, the couple is paying good money for the band to entertain enthusiastically. They are hoping for this to be the best day of their lives (so far). Why would they want some hipster bass player rolling his eyes while he jogs his way through "Proud Mary"? Bassist Bill wouldn't want that attitude for his wedding, so why is he putting that vibe out for Steve and Sally?

I need the non-musicians (we call you civilians) to check back in now and pay attention.

The message here is to be respectful to the client and eager to meet their requests.

Just because it's routine to you doesn't mean you need to show it. The poster for my show is critical to me, Mr. Office Max guy. My package is important to me, Miss Post Office lady. My health is vital to me, Dr. Dude. Be considerate of my state of mind, my time, and my project—you are paid to do so.

I was discussing this concept with a friend of mine in the watch business. I asked him to identify the equivalent to the "wedding gig" or the "lower rung" endeavors in his field. He said, "battery replacements and watch sizing." Yes, the constant parade of dead watches and making sure they fit just right maintains a continuous inflow. This service is integral to a profitable watch business. However, this constant stream can become mundane. Batteries and sizings are also void of the cachet and excitement one swells with from selling a Rolex. He pointed out the importance of detailed and quality customer service on these mundane tasks. He added, "You take care of a customer enough times, you become *their guy*. When they need a graduation gift or anniversary present, we get the call."

It would seem to serve us all to identify the "wedding gigs" in our professional affairs. Can you? How are you responding?

Just remember, you will sustain relationships and a client base longer if you fight the urge to downplay and minimize routine service requests. These requests are routine for you but quite meaningful to those asking. (Seriously, if I have to play "Hotel California" one more time, I'm gonna shove my mic in my ear! But not really. I'm aware that it's meaningful to you, and I'm going to gladly play it for you, brother. *"On a dark desert highway. A Shure mic in my ear..."*)

If you take on an endeavor, be respectful—be professional.

HOOK #68

Whenever you are able,
hire a roadie.

FOR MANY YEARS I worked with a close friend and mentor who insisted I hire a crew to set up my gear on all performances where she was the coordinator.

Her thought was that the client was hiring a "star" performer, and that image needed reinforcement from the moment I was first visible at the event. I'm not above setting up my own gear. However, having a crew does lend to the idea that the operation is a step up.

My manager tells the story of the time he was on a show with a famous comedian. When arriving at the hotel, the comedian insisted on going to his room and changing out of his casual attire before entering the ballroom to meet the band and client—he even strategically carried a cocktail glass to complete his branded image.

One more example from my manager involves a fellow act on the record label. For load in, this particular band leader would dress in baggy clothes and a big floppy hat that covered his face so no one could see him loading in gear. Legend holds he would even go by a different name during load in.

The audience wants the performer to be a star. Help reinforce that image with a crew.

Another benefit is that you can focus on other tasks.

I cannot overemphasize how many times having my crew load in my gear was essential to the show getting off to a good start. My trusted crew chief, Stephen Boye, has loaded in my piano hundreds of times over the years. His work has allowed me to converse with the client, manage the band, prepare my thoughts for the show, or take on any other random requirements that arise. I've also shielded myself from the aggravation brought on by hauling gear through hallways, stairs, alleys, and stages.

As I write this now, I am preparing for an upcoming show. Unfortunately, it would not be prudent to hire a crew due to the limited budget. Without a crew, part of my strategy this week centers around the transportation and load in of my equipment. It is a necessary distraction. But a distraction, nonetheless.

I believe the overall theme here is the importance of delegating responsibilities.

Sure, I enjoy negotiating deals and drafting contracts. I don't mind keeping the books and managing the calendars. I'd rather not haul the gear, but I can and do so when prudent. All that being said, these are tasks others can do for my business if needed. The true essence of Matt Wilson Entertainment comes from the ideas, strategy, and direction. Ultimately, the creative vision must come from me to separate my business from all the rest.

> ## "Any time I can focus on the purest of my responsibilities, the greater MWE has a chance to meet its goal."

Any time I can focus on the purest of my responsibilities (writing, image, direction, and show arrangement), the greater MWE has a chance to meet its goal. That goal being Matt Wilson Entertainment, not Bob Wilson Entertainment or Jane Wilson Entertainment, or pick a name that's not me.

I'm sure we can all relate in some way. For example, when I'm working on calendars or contracts, I allow my environment to be chaotic. The phone is on and nearby. Text and email alerts are engaged and audible. The office door is open, and there might be the news on the tube or some sports talk on the radio. In these moments, I'm the manager of MWE, and my focus is wide.

However, when I'm writing, practicing, arranging a song, editing a video, or any other creative matter, I close myself off to the outside world and all of its distractions. As manager, I have delegated Matt to his number one job. "Go make something, Matt!" "Tell us where we are going next, Matt!" "What are we gonna give them, Matt?"

To write the best song or book, or edit the coolest video, or outline the next awesome show, I need a clear and fixated focus. That focus is easier to access if I'm not loading a fifty-pound keyboard into a van. Not impossible, just easier.

A counselor once suggested I observe the coordination between someone in a position of power and their entourage. This particular counselor was an expert on the mind and social interactions. He explained that those carrying the bags and opening the doors for the CEO or president were not only doing so as a matter of respect or duty, but also to create an environment for the leader to have that targeted focus I mentioned earlier. Believe it or not, opening a door can be a distraction. (I'm recalling that ongoing, funny bit in the Will Ferrell and Zach Galifianakis movie, *The Campaign*, in which someone was exiting a room, and they couldn't work the doorknob. Those in the room would say things like "Jiggle it and pull up," or "Push down and then pull to the right." We've all been there! Funny!)

Anyway, the delegation of responsibilities creates an environment for focus and greater productivity.

If it's in the budget, find some help with your stuff. You will have a free mind, maintain an image, and you'll be creating a job to boot!

HOOK #69

Momentum is real.
Initial success is
often pivotal for ambition
and opportunity.

WE ARE ALL aware that the first impression is the most important. Although nothing is absolute every time, it seems logical that the first encounter you have with someone, or something, will significantly influence opinions moving forward.

A new artist I once managed was finding some success in his budding career, yet he'd also experienced some failures with a few venues in the local area. I made it clear we could not afford to spoil his name with many other venues in town. I was confident opportunities would present themselves, but we would typically only have one chance to capitalize. Yes, we were eager to set things in motion; however, we would be doing way more harm than good if not rehearsed and prepared.

I'm sure you've heard the adage: "Those who have more, get more." This has been proven again and again in business. The opposite of this saying can be true also. If those who have more are getting more, we can then suppose that those who don't have more are probably not getting much at all, comparatively. This is a complex problem for society; yet in business affairs, it's regarded as the risk one takes for trying.

I think a fascinating example of this is in the music industry. There are millions of working musicians, yet only a small fraction amasses a great amount of *more* fortune and *more* fame. For every Alicia Keys or Bono, there are a million other, not as successful, singers and bands. A more realistic view is that for every full-time working musician, there are thousands who must have other careers or supplemental streams of income.

I see the momentum of "more getting more" at a local level in my business all the time. There are instances where a cover band (a band that plays other people's music—a wedding band is a perfect example) becomes so popular that they decide to form a separate identical group to perform when there is a conflict of availability. Rather than the client looking to another band entirely (spreading the wealth and opportunity), they book the second-tier group from the most popular brand.

It looks like this:

- Dance Town becomes the most requested wedding band in town.
- Dance Town forms Dance City to cover the overwhelming number of booking inquires.
- Dance Town's brand and market share become greater than any other band in town. More, getting more. Momentum, baby!

So, what do we do? How do we elevate ourselves to the "more, get more" rank? How do we generate momentum? Here are two things to consider when starting a new venture or project:

1. Are you really prepared? Be objective!
2. Did you identify momentum as a goal?

It is most critical to build momentum in the beginning. If I perform at a venue for the first time and do an adequate-to-great job, then I should be asked back at some point. It may not be immediately, or even in the near future. However, the door is open. If I do a poor job, then the door is closed. Done. Happens every time!

For those just starting, a few closed doors and you will have to find a new market. These doors are not immune to the theories above. The more doors you open, the more doors there are to open. A few closed doors, and you run out of doors.

I know there are plenty of examples where one overcomes a bad first impression or capitalizes on a second or third chance. Yet, these scenarios are not guaranteed and seem less likely. All business is hard and competitive. Don't make it harder by ignoring the value of building momentum from the start.

Be as certain as possible that you are prepared before you present to the market. Be purposeful in an approach that includes building momentum for the future.

HOOK #70

Determine the most efficient way to allocate your most valuable resources.

MY OPINION HOLDS that the three most valuable resources in any business are talent, money, and time.

I recall setting and prioritizing goals with one of my artists. We laid out the goals by identifying the desired outcome—he wanted more paid performances. To do that, we needed to increase his exposure. To do that, he needed to establish an online presence. So, the immediate goal began to come into focus. Goal = more gigs = more exposure = online presence = website.

As we dove further, we recognized the website needed new promotional material (photos and videos). So, the immediate goal became even more defined. We also determined he needed some equipment for performances.

As is the case for any small business, his resources were limited, and he needed to prioritize one goal at a time. Someone with unlimited funds can be haphazard when prioritizing spending; this is not the case for those on a tight budget. So, I suggested we create the promotional material before we buy equipment for the gigs we don't have and won't have until we produce material to solicit the desired performances. Why buy equipment for shows you don't have and can't market? (You can always find equipment in a pinch.)

Also, the sooner we opened his "store," the sooner we could move on with the business of selling. Buying the equipment prematurely would have provided his business with idle resources.

So, we aimed (money) his effort (talent) in the direction of taking photos, shooting a video, and building a website first (time). This proved to be the most efficient path.

Fast forward six months. After the website, photos, and video were complete, we revisited the equipment idea. To be clear, the equipment was always needed. It was just a matter of deciding the best time to invest our resources (money).

There is also a physical component to the talent resource. For example, I have to be mindful of how and when I use my voice. As a singer, I can get in hot water if I'm not sensitive to vocal fatigue. Hours talking on the phone doing business is counterproductive on a day when I need to sing for a few hours later that night.

Also, there is the issue of hats. We all wear a multitude of "hats" in our professional and personal lives. Whatever hat you are wearing should control where your mind is focused. As a writer, I must decide to put on the writer hat (talent) and set aside time to write—even when there are equally important tasks waiting. (When any of us say, "I didn't have time," what we are really saying is "I didn't *take* time.") As a business owner, I must consciously decide to put away the distractions and invest (time) in my talent through writing or practicing. This investment of my time and talent should produce results that the guy wearing the business hat will approve (money).

How can you allocate the most valuable resources in your affairs? These three steps can be useful:

1. Identify the **Talent** (product). What are you selling?

2. Take stock of your resources available to promote and move the Talent along. (**Money** or some sort of substitute, like bartering.)

3. Determine where your **Time** and resources should be allocated first. I suggest you invest in what will most effectively showcase the Talent and produce the most immediate return. Remember, momentum in business is real (Hook #69).

Good luck!

HOOK #71

Be easy to find.
When someone
wants your services,
they will let you know.

FOR YEARS I would vent my frustration to my manager and agent about the leads that came through the website. Someone would fill out the form and ask about our services. To me, that meant that they wanted to hire the band. After our initial response, I wanted a follow-up soon after.

It became clear over time that these were just "shopping around" inquiries, no different than someone shopping for a shirt at Macy's. A quick look over the shirts draws your interest. Then you take one off the rack and hold it up. Maybe you are still intrigued, and you finally look at the price tag. If the shirt meets all of your qualifications, then you probably buy it.

However, if it doesn't, you hang it back up and move on. You certainly don't return a few days later to tell the salesperson you bought a shirt elsewhere. Also, you do not desire a follow-up from the store about your interest in the shirt. To exhaust this analogy, if you decide later you want the shirt, you will go back to the store and buy it of your own volition.

I cannot think of a scenario where, in the middle of a show or an event, the talent buyer would say, "Oh, we were talking with the Matt Wilson Band and forgot to book them!"

I don't want to be dismissive here. Following up with potential clients is an accepted and expected strategy in business. Most companies with sales departments *require* the sales team to follow up. Stats prove that persistence pays off in most industries. I sort the follow-up in the "be accessible and easy to find" category. There are also statistics on how and when you should follow up with your lead. Follow up to your heart's content!

However, my experience leads me to believe a follow-up may serve as a gentle reminder and an action item but will rarely function as a means of persuasion. (Unless you are offering something extra or lowering your price.) I've also found that time and energy aimed at repeatedly following up can prove to be wasted efforts. And, chasing clients who are just not interested might cause you to unnecessarily change your product. I believe when they want you, they will respond. This has been proven to me, time and time again.

To challenge my opinion and approach, I reached out to a few sales professionals. I learned that each valued the follow-up with varied tactics and views, yet they all asked why it mattered. I explained that I had spent many working hours fretting and laboring over lost leads when I could have been looking forward to creating new opportunities.

Through these discussions, I found there must be a balance. So, another list! **I offer these suggestions below to, hopefully, relieve some stress about acquiring new business and managing your time.**

1. Be accessible and easy to find. (Websites, social media, print media, marketing, advertising—Location, Location, Location!)

2. Be respectful of the form of communication the client has requested. Don't force a phone call if they prefer email, etc.

3. Focus your efforts on the first sales presentation. Give your best while you have their attention. Be punctual, professional, and informative. Don't rely on the follow-up.

4. Determine the amount of effort to invest in the follow-up strategy and streamline your procedure. Consider the probability of making the sale and the overall potential gain. If low on both fronts, let it go.

5. Don't stress about someone who has gone radio silent. Maybe they are still considering. Perhaps they are not interested. Are you satisfied with your product and sales pitch? If so…

6. Move on. Know that moving on will not hurt your chances if they change their mind.

The information shared here is just the tip of the iceberg. I'm not a sales guru. However, my goal is to encourage you to look forward to new opportunities, generate enthusiasm, and gain momentum. Revisiting stale leads can be an obstacle to creativity and enterprise.

HOOK #72

A performance motivated by money alone will suffer.

AS A YOUNG man, I told my mother that if I could make a living as a professional musician, I would consider my career successful. That statement is still true. I have been a full-time musician for almost thirty years now, and I'm quite proud of my achievement. However, I don't feel completely satisfied. There are plenty of artistic goals I still hold on to and dream of accomplishing.

My growing list of responsibilities has altered my career path. The most significant change in my life has been becoming a father. My financial needs and goals, along with my desire to "be around," have compelled me to focus on more profitable and local endeavors.

That being said, I have noticed in cases where the financial return is the only motivation on a performance or job, I am unfulfilled. And the performance suffers.

> *"...in cases where the financial return is the only motivation on a performance, I am unfulfilled. And the performance suffers."*

I think it's within our human nature to, at times, take a job for granted. Finding out *why* is not the focus here. **I would propose that a job just for money does not provide meaning. Meaning is critical to motivation.**

I once shared a Tuesday night gig with a buddy of mine. The gig paid "weekend money" and was in town. Some nights, when the venue wasn't as full as usual, he would slack off during the show. On many occasions, I reminded him that having a regular, well-paying, Tuesday night gig was invaluable to a working musician. We needed to be mindful of this and always do our best. Acknowledging the value of the gig was not enough for him. He needed more motivation. His performances continued to fluctuate between good and bad, based on the attendance.

So, what do I do when the income is the main reason for taking the job? I adjust my focus. Every performance, I aim to sing and play to the best of my ability. I aim to look good, sound good, and be good (Hook #79). I take the venue, money, and audience out of the equation. Remember, if you take the gig, do what is required and expected to perform the gig (Hook #9).

So yes, I take gigs because I need the income. It's my livelihood. However, my motivation is something greater. My motivation is to be a professional, maintain my skill level, sustain brand momentum, and be respectful to the venues and clients. Most importantly, I strive to give the audience a positive and memorable experience.

If you find you are only doing something for money, reevaluate, and focus on more meaningful motives.

HOOK #73

The product you invest your time in and sell is the product you are. Is the product you are what you want to be?

HAVE YOU EVER noticed someone's Facebook or Instagram post on a recent career success and wondered, "Why not me too?" This is a common occurrence, I'm sure. Maybe there's an answer.

To this day, my manager emphasizes that my songwriting ability persuaded him the most to take me on as a client. I'd prefer the public and my peers also recognize me for my songwriting first and foremost. So far, I have not aimed to focus solely on or commit to pursuing my original music.

I never really had aspirations for Broadway. Yet, when the opportunity presented itself, I sharpened my skills and landed the part in *Movin' Out*. After leaving the show, I was searching for direction and a job. It made sense to parlay my experience in *Movin' Out* into future performances. Soon after, I was performing in the piano bar scene again and playing with my band. I believed I could insert my original music alongside Billy Joel covers and dance music.

The long road that accompanies pursuing a songwriting career couldn't compete with the band's success as a private event and club band. So, to stay competitive in the market, I invested time and resources into the cover band.

More and more, the band became recognized as a cover band, and for the most part, the original music was left unnoticed. I continued to make records and videos with my original music. I continued to play the original songs with the band during most of our shows. Still, the business of the band was driven by our ability to entertain as a cover act. My songs were not completely lost in the shuffle; however, they were always at the bottom of the deck. To this day, the Matt Wilson Band enthusiastically plays private events and clubs as a cover band. We genuinely enjoy entertaining, and I no longer fight the band's image being a cover act.

For so long, I struggled with the lack of attention I was receiving for my songs. One day, I realized my expectations were misguided. I was receiving exactly what I was putting in. The business version of you reap what you sow. I wanted the band to be recognized for the original music. However, I put more resources into promoting what was most successful and more predictable—cover music. Not a bad business plan! Yet not an effective strategy for a songwriter.

I've come to terms with the Matt Wilson Band being a cover band that also plays a little bit of original music. I'm satisfied with our chosen path. However, to bring life to my songs, I am exploring other avenues for exposure. I can continue to reap the rewards of the time and energy my bandmates and I have invested in the Matt Wilson Band without bearing the mental weight of being something we are not. All the while, I can steer my songwriting goals in a different direction.

I wouldn't have been able to reconcile this dilemma without the idea that **the product you invest your time in and sell is the product you are.**

Unless I'm confident I've put in the dedicated effort, I no longer ask, "Why not me?"

HOOK #74

Look forward with HOW,
not backward with WHY.

AS A BUSINESS owner and manager, I am ultimately responsible for an efficient operation. Although I delegate tasks, I must manage them closely or from afar, and take responsibility for their completion.

When things don't go according to plan, I've found it's a waste of time to spend too much effort on *why*.

Yes, having an understanding of *why* there was a breakdown is relevant. However, the sooner I can move on to *how* we can improve, the better. I see *how* as far more efficient than *why*.

A band, like any other group or business, will encounter a multitude of concerns. What songs are we playing, when is the rehearsal, where and what time is the gig, what are we wearing, how much are we getting paid, when are we getting paid, will there be food (Hook #58), and the list goes on. From a manager's perspective, within each of these common matters, there is room for aggravation. Members are late and don't know the material. Vendors are uncertain of the agreed-upon payment or are slow when paying. Venues are in disrepair, poorly run, and understaffed. Again, the list seems unlimited.

Solving the problem of *how* things can be better next time propels the discussion forward. *Why* is accusatory and demands reasoning. *How* can be presented, simply, as a better way.

For example, rather than ask the drummer why his tempos are off all the time, we can implement a metronome to our production. Let the metronome set the tempo at the beginning of the tune rather than rely on one player's memory and feel. Or, if the band is typically late, there is little reason to fret over why. As a manager, you simply set the load in time earlier, remind the band of traffic concerns, plan minor rehearsals for soundcheck, or stress that being on time is critical to the client. Think forward, not backward.

Why is a breeding ground for arguments and discord. *How* removes the discussion and calmly sets the new rule.

Aiming at *how* will more than likely answer *why*. Managers, trust me, if someone has a problem with the new standards, they will tell you *why*. Change the *how*, and everyone must adapt. Often, the issues will correct themselves without the drama that accompanies the *why* discussion.

How also puts the responsibility back in the hands of the managers and decision-makers. Relying on the care and attention to detail from those hired to promote and deliver the vision is careless. Sure, there are those on the team who want only the best for the project. However, no one will care more than the creator or owner. (I've learned that if I don't seem to care, then the band won't care.)

If you have ever been responsible for a child, you will understand that this management tactic is mandatory.

Ask a kid *why* something happened, and you will simply get "it was an accident." To them, that's sufficient reasoning.

"Why didn't you do your homework?"

"I accidentally forgot."

The real reason was, of course, video games, television, or toys. A right-minded parent wouldn't spend too much time reasoning with the child; they would just move on to setting new rules about homework and playing with the iPad.

Most of us don't grow up; we just get older. The rules of *how* help us stay in line and act responsibly.

Without "how rules," we would all be wandering aimlessly and perpetually failing.

By accident, of course.

In the famous words of Billy Joel, "Don't Ask Me Why."

CREATIVITY

Getting better at making stuff

HOOK #75

Nurture your ideas.
Give them a chance
to grow.

THERE ARE FEW ideas *not* worth trying—this is a ground rule for musicians recording a new project in the studio. Of course, time and budget play a role in determining how experimental you can afford to be. That said, do your best to follow your creative mind and see where it takes you.

Don't be a gatekeeper to inspiration. At some point, you will need to determine the idea's usefulness, but not in the beginning. I've written many songs I found dull while composing. Fully aware the song wasn't meeting its potential, I saved the evaluation for down the road. As time passed, a new perspective inspired a rewrite and something better and more enjoyable emerged.

Here is how I apply this Hook:

1. I **welcome** all creative ideas.
2. I **pursue** them until they are complete, or I run out of inspiration.
3. I **save**—finished or not. Someday, they may be of value.

HOOK #76

*Be patient and reasonable with your goals.
The developmental process is critical.*

IN THE SUMMER of 2016, I was going through some career changes. I had just ended a long-term business relationship. (Truthfully, you could say I was fired, but that would be too simple an explanation, and who wants to say, "I was fired.") I began to question if it was time to do something radically different with my talents. I started reading, praying, writing, learning to play guitar, exploring my existence with my therapist, and giving all thoughts equal time to be considered.

Over a two- or three-day span that summer, a wave of inspiration flooded my mind. These "Hooks" you are taking in and considering poured out and into my iPhone within just a few short days. I did not question why I was writing these things down, nor did I ignore them or view the process as a waste of time.

Back in 2014, I explored the idea of creating a seminar focusing on performing through anxiety. I realized that my summer of 2016 inspiration was a continuation of, and connected to, my work from 2014.

I type these words now in the fall of 2018. I will not speculate on the date this will be available for anyone to read and possibly find useful (I'm editing and proofreading in the fall of 2020). However, I know that since that first bit of inspiration, I have grown and gained more wisdom and experience. I'm positive that being patient with this writing is just as important as finishing.

Consider your ideas, projects, and even relationships like a newly planted tree. If you have grand plans for that tree, it will take some time to grow a solid foundation. The grandest of treehouses and high-flying swings can only be supported by long limbs and a robust trunk. Think of the treehouse or swing as your expectations. Attaching a swing to or constructing a house in an underdeveloped tree is an effort doomed for disappointment and pain. Worst of all, you are left with a crushed tree!

Rushed expectations can lead to unrealized and unfulfilled dreams.

The development is crucial to the final outcome.

HOOK #77

Choose an environment that inspires.
Read, listen, and watch for what moves you.

AS I HAVE mentioned before, routine is essential to relationships, performance, and creativity. I rely on routine and do my best to follow my script.

One of my daily routines involves listening to the radio. Sometimes I choose music, but mainly I dial in some sort of talk radio: sports, news, politics, or a podcast. Over time, I observed that my selection influenced my thoughts. I now use this realization to my advantage.

I know that if I want to write music, I should listen to music that inspires me. If I want to work on my book, I will listen to a philosophy, religion, or psychology podcast or lecture. If I need encouragement, I will listen to the words of my pastors or counselors.

We think about what we see, hear, and read. This is why our daily jobs and responsibilities primarily consume our thoughts.

Even if you just want to shut everything down for a moment and relax, be purposeful when choosing what you see, hear, and read.

You can control how and when you are inspired.

HOOK #78

*When the creative muse
comes calling,
give her your attention.
Rarely does she
repeat herself.*

ALL FAMOUS WRITERS have some sort of recording device on hand at all times. I can't prove this statement. However, in every interview I've listened to featuring a writer, they've referenced the recorder on the bedside table or the easy and immediate access to a pen, a pad, etc. (So, that should suffice to support my claim.) Plus, smartphones!

CREATIVE MEMORY TEST

Let's conduct an experiment. Take a few moments to create something: a song, a story outline, a drawing, whatever. Now find a way to document it with a recorder or write it down immediately. For the sake of this experiment, don't focus on memorizing it or remembering it. Just focus on creating and documenting. Now put it away. In a day or two, come back and recreate the same song or story precisely the way you did before, without referencing the recording or notes. My bet is that you cannot.

Imagine, now, that this inspiration comes calling in the middle of the night or at a stoplight. It will come, and it will go. **Only once will a writer feel the frustration of trying to recall that great idea before they will no longer leave the recall to memory alone.**

Being a writer takes discipline. Sometimes that means stopping whatever you are doing to take the muse's call. She's a terrible friend. She only comes around every now and then, unannounced, and at weird times of the day. She often speaks quietly and gives you only one chance to hear. She's unreliable and cannot be reached when you beckon. However, when she's around, and you are paying attention, she will fill you up with light and hope and joy.

I do believe we can be creative without a muse. You can learn to channel your creativity and you should. However, there are those special moments when the idea seems divine. I believe they are.

Be sensitive to these moments. (Don't forget to press record!)

HOOK #79

Look good,
sound good,
and be good!

MY AIM FOR every performance is to look good, sound good, and be good.

LOOK GOOD

People enjoy watching someone who looks the part. Remember, the audience listens with their eyes!

I wear clothes I believe match my performance style. I call it "stage black." Black clothes look good onstage, and typically, you can't go wrong with stage black. All my clothes are cool, but not hip. And they are black. I wear a suit jacket—black. I figure I'm a no-nonsense, straightforward, no-frills entertainer, so that's how I dress. I prefer my clothes to not get in my way.

I do take into consideration the venue and occasion. So, sometimes the stage black is not as appropriate. If I'm playing a cocktail set at the Four Seasons, I'll wear some color, but still no frills. No distractions. No "Why did I wear this?" going through my head while I'm performing.

One year I was performing on Halloween, and I put on a dress, a black wig, a pearl necklace, and painted my face like a jack-o'-lantern. I was "Jackie-O'-Lantern." (Did you just laugh? You laughed a little, I know.) Clever costume, for sure! But after the first tune, the excitement wore off, and I realized I was stuck wearing a dress, wig, and pumpkin makeup for the next five hours. I swore I would never do something like that again! For me, my stage clothes are simple, comfortable, and cool (not hip). And black (usually).

I also aim to take care of myself so that I maintain my physical appearance. Feeling confident in the way I look contributes to my ability to perform at my best. At the very least, I won't be distracted by a poor choice of clothing or appearing unintentionally disheveled. Nor will my audience be distracted by my appearance. I aim to *look good*.

SOUND GOOD

The average audience member can't hear the intricacies of perfect pitch, tempos, chord voicings, and correct song arrangements. They can, however, discern what simply sounds good.

Should I play louder or softer? What key should I play the song in? A lower key generally allows me to sing quieter (closer to my speaking voice), whereas a higher key requires more volume and air. Should I sing in a breathy, intimate tone, or should I sing boldly, attacking, and hard?

What is the mood of the room? Am I responsible for setting the mood of the room? Playing the song that fits the vibe goes a long way towards whether my listener thinks I sound good. Although there might be a flat note or wrong chord, my most important thought is, "Does the overall sound come together to make a pleasing experience?" Whatever the case, I aim to *sound good*.

BE GOOD

Just as I don't want my appearance to create a distraction, I also do not want my behavior to be a distraction. I've learned the hard way that even the actions of a rock star can have negative consequences. I am a professional, and most people I work with want me to act accordingly.

Be on time. Know my part. Have my equipment. Be agreeable, positive, and kind. Show some enthusiasm for the show. Set personal problems aside during the performance. Be focused. Be good.

Being good also means to set a professional standard. Although the audience might not know that some notes are flat, tempos rushed, or chords are wrong, I do, and it matters to me. I've learned not to let these things distract me during my performance, but I do mark the errors to revisit later. Merely aiming to please the crowd dilutes the performance and eliminates any motivation for quality control. Sure, my performance may entertain the audience, but that doesn't mean my effort was professionally adequate or to the best of my ability. Aiming to perform at my best, technically, keeps me engaged and challenged. It shows that not only am I concerned about the listener's experience (Are they entertained?), but I'm also concerned about the quality in which I am entertaining. In all facets of a performance, I aim to *be good*.

This is what I've learned about how to be a professional onstage.

HOOK #80

FIGHT to stay inspired!

THIS MISERABLE, UNFAIR, annoying, brutal world was built to beat you down and, ultimately, kill you. It is what it is, folks.

However, it was also made to nurture, produce life, lend support, and inspire. Fight for that!

Pure inspiration gives hope, peace, joy, excitement, and love. **Fight for that! Seek it out. Build an environment that welcomes inspiration.**

As children, we were quite selfish with our time. We were on a constant quest for what triggered our fun button and rid us of the boredom. When the TV or video games were not available, we would create our own stories and worlds to conquer. The stuffed animals and He-Man action figures embodied all that was needed to burn an hour or two. We were determined to change our state of boredom. We became inspired.

Fight for that!

What gets you excited? What moves you? Be around that.

How can you fight for inspiration? Make it a priority.

1. **Set aside a dedicated time for creativity.** When I am able, I focus on my creative efforts in the early part of the day. Before I let the world fall on top of me through email, phone, and Facebook, I fill my thoughts with whatever I want to create. More often than not, this time is the most rewarding, and I have a better day for it.

2. **Heighten your creative senses.** I once derailed a business conversation because the guy said something that sounded like an idea for a song. I pointed out the catchy turn of phrase, and within an hour, I wrote the song. I'm always on alert for ideas.

3. **Get emotional! Reject cynicism and burnout.** Play, laugh, cry, reminisce. Remember, Peter Pan couldn't fly in his business suit.

"Peter Pan couldn't fly in his business suit."

In case you don't remember or don't know, the old Proverb says, "A joyful heart is good medicine, but a crushed spirit dries up the bones."

True inspiration brings me joy every time—and that's worth the fight!

THE ENCORE

I'M SURE YOU are all aware of a song I wrote years ago called "Middle Me" (wink). The theme centers around the idea that we all have a "younger me," "middle me," and "older me." The song reveals the introspection of "middle me" looking back at "younger me."

Middle me

look at younger me

look at that smile

look at that hair

all that drive

going everywhere

middle me

look at younger me

makin' those plans

stirring a dream

hitting the town

just to be seen

middle me

look at younger me

fallin' in love

with the wrong girls

breaking the hearts

breaking the rules

middle me

look at younger me

a little too vain

a little too dumb

a little bit of work

a whole lotta fun

thinking 'bout the days of younger me

something 'bout the days of younger me

man, I miss those days of younger me

Like most, sometimes I'm troubled by small battles with regret. I'm confronted with the reality that I was not better when I was younger. Better at what? You name it. When you have the luxury to see how it all turned out, you are inclined to want to go back and do it all again, but better this time. Make a few changes, yes?

Any time I get bogged down in this burdensome and intrusive thinking, I always come back to two conclusions:

1. I always cared and wanted for the best. There are many reasons our actions do not line up with our intentions. Some reasons are excuses, and some reasons are legitimate barriers. Whatever the case, "younger me" cared and tried. I never started the day with the thought, "Hey, let's really screw things up!" That matters to me now. I'd have trouble accepting that some of my regrets are the consequences of an immature knothead who didn't give a rip.

2. Everything I have, I've earned through hard work, perseverance,
confidence, courage, and the grace of God. I'm fortunate and
grateful to have the experiences I now tuck away in my life's
tome—and they are many. Yes, at times I could have given
more effort, studied more, gone to bed earlier, and buttoned
one more button on my shirt. Yet, the immaturity of a young
rock star must run its course. I know this sounds a bit dismissive
and rationalizing. However, it's true. So, maybe "younger me"
was a knothead, at times. A knothead who cared and enjoyed life
while pursuing a calling. Even though not entirely applicable,
I recall what my manager, Mike Mordecai, said about retirement:
"I was retired until I was about thirty-seven, and then I went
to work."

So, now what? Once I remind myself that I haven't wasted my life away, I
realize I have planes to catch, shows to perform, emails to answer, books to
write, records to release, a wife to love, and two boys to raise. I'm nowhere
near done with this thing.

Whatever regrets I harbor about being a better musician, singer, husband,
father, businessman, or writer are aimed at "younger me." Even if "younger
me" was "yesterday me," I still have all the time in the world to get this
thing right!

And, even if I don't get it right, ultimately, I won't know the difference. (I'm
not going to spell this out for you.)

I wrote in my song "Love Loan":

You can't take it with you, that's what they say.

So we might as well all spend free.

I'm gonna spend what's been tendered in love

and the end, I'm gonna take it all with me.

The idea that we can't take our possessions to the grave also applies to our regrets and fears. Our goals. Our dreams. The truth is, all that stuff evaporates in the wind. I'm saying that we can, and should, aim high and run hard until we can't. Or aim low and run easy. Whatever, man, just don't act or live like you are done until you are done.

I asked some friends and family to read this book and offer feedback. These dear readers pointed out that I didn't end the book—no wrap-up. Well, here you go...

WRAPPING UP

IF YOU READ *Hooks* and identified with anything presented, you must be in a place of wanting to improve or gain insight. (Or you agreed to do me a favor. Thanks, y'all!) Ok, cool.

What are you going to do with it all? I hope my experiences can bring you comfort and peace. I hope you understand that you are not alone in your thoughts and fears. My aim is that my successes and missteps along the way give you a model to follow or a pitfall to avoid.

So...

Sing better today. Write better today. Play with your kids a little longer today. Be kind to the irritating customer service rep today. Goof off today. Practice today. Look your best today. Compliment someone today. Accept that you are not entirely defined by your work today. Raise your Base Level today. Don't be preoccupied with the passing trees on the side of the highway today. Don't get bogged down in assigning value today. Take in all the moments today. Accept earned confidence today. Realize that you are courageous because you face the fear today. Plan for a future, and live it today. Today.

Press on, y'all.

Made in the USA
Columbia, SC
10 August 2021